From Scientific Psychology to the Study of Persons

This is a critical, personalized approach to reframing the discipline of psychology through a singular narrative in the form of a memoir written by a successful research psychologist.

In this book we follow Martin's unique career, which has allowed him to understand and adopt different perspectives and ways of approaching psychology, from working in applied areas like educational and counseling psychology to more specialized areas like theory and history of psychology. His journey through and within the field describes his movement away from scientifically based psychology, which views teachings and interventions to be primarily underwritten by hard scientific evidence. Martin exposes the flaws in this approach and highlights the importance of focusing on the study of persons in their life contexts over the use of aggregated group results to ensure that the discipline survives and flourishes.

This is an impactful and universally applicable book with valuable insights for students and scholars of psychology today, particularly those studying history of psychology, theoretical psychology, and philosophical psychology.

Jack Martin is a Fellow of the Canadian and American Psychological Associations, former President of the Society for Theoretical and Philosophical Psychology (STPP), and recipient of the STPP's Award for Distinguished Lifetime Contributions to Theoretical and Philosophical Psychology.

Advances in Theoretical and Philosophical Psychology

Series Editor

Brent D. Slife
Brigham Young University

Editorial Board

The Hidden Worldviews of Psychology's Theory, Research, and Practice
Brent D. Slife, Kari A. O'Grady, and Russell D. Kosits

On Hijacking Science
Exploring the Nature and Consequences of Overreach in Psychology
Edwin E. Gantt and Richard N. Williams

Situating Qualitative Methods in Psychological Science
Brian Schiff

Hermeneutic Moral Realism in Psychology
Theory and Practice
Brent D. Slife and Stephen Yanchar

A Humanities Approach to the Psychology of Personhood
Jeff Sugarman and Jack Martin

Subjectivity in Psychology in the Era of Social Justice
Bethany Morris, Chase O'Gwin, Sebastienne Grant, Sakenya McDonald

The Ethical Visions of Psychotherapy
Kevin Smith

Therapeutic Ethics in Context and in Dialogue
Kevin Smith

A Multidisciplinary Approach to Embodiment
Understanding Human Being
Nancy K. Dess

From Scientific Psychology to the Study of Persons
A Psychologist's Memoir
Jack Martin

https://www.routledge.com/psychology/series/TPP

From Scientific Psychology to the Study of Persons

A Psychologist's Memoir

Jack Martin

NEW YORK AND LONDON

First published 2021
by Routledge
52 Vanderbilt Avenue, New York, NY 10017

and by Routledge
2 Park Square, Milton Park, Abingdon, Oxon, OX14 4RN

Routledge is an imprint of the Taylor & Francis Group, an informa business

Library of Congress Cataloging-in-Publication Data
A catalog record for this title has been requested

ISBN: 978-0-367-55012-7 (hbk)
ISBN: 978-0-367-55294-7 (pbk)
ISBN: 978-1-003-09285-8 (ebk)

Typeset in Times New Roman
by Deanta Global Publishing Services, Chennai, India

FOR WYN

Contents

Series Foreword

Brent D. Slife, Editor

Psychologists need to face the facts. Their commitment to empiricism for answering disciplinary questions does not prevent pivotal questions from arising that cannot be evaluated exclusively through empirical methods, hence the title of this series: *Advances in Theoretical and Philosophical Psychology*. Such moral questions as, "What is the nature of a good life?" are crucial to psychotherapists but are not answerable through empirical methods alone. And what of the methods themselves? Many have worried that our current psychological means of investigation are not adequate for fully understanding the person (e.g., Schiff, 2019). How do we address this concern through empirical methods without running headlong into the dilemma of methods investigating themselves? Such questions are in some sense philosophical, to be sure, but the discipline of psychology cannot advance even its own empirical agenda without addressing questions like these in defensible ways.

How then should the discipline of psychology deal with such distinctly theoretical questions? We could leave the answers exclusively to professional philosophers, but this option would mean that the conceptual foundations of the discipline, including the conceptual framework of empiricism itself, are left to scholars who are *outside* the discipline. As undoubtedly helpful as philosophers are and would be, this situation would mean that the people doing the actual psychological work, psychologists themselves, are divorced from the people who formulate and re-formulate the conceptual foundations of that work. This division of labor would not seem to serve the long-term viability of the discipline.

Instead, the founders of psychology—thinkers such as Wundt, Freud, and James—recognized the importance of psychologists in formulating their own foundations. These parents of psychology not only did their own theorizing, in cooperation with many other disciplines; they realized the significance of psychologists continuously *re*-examining these theories and philosophies. This re-examination process allowed for the people most directly involved in and knowledgeable about the discipline to be the ones to decide *whether* changes were needed and *how* such changes would best be implemented. This book series is dedicated to that task, the examining and re-examining of psychology's foundations.

Acknowledgments

This memoir owes everything to my many teachers, students, colleagues, and co-workers whose cumulative contributions have made my life and career in psychology possible.

In particular, I want to recognize my good friend and closest colleague, Jeff Sugarman. I thank him for his unstinting support, willing collaboration, and enormous generosity.

I have dedicated this memoir to my wife and best friend, Wyn. It would be folly to attempt to state here what she means to me.

The publication of this memoir would not have been possible without the encouragement and support of series editor Brent Slife, Routledge editor Lucy McClune, and assistant editor Akshita Pattiyani.

1 My Life in Psychology
An Introduction

Psychology claims to help people understand and improve themselves and their lives based on scientific knowledge about human beings and their functioning. Psychologists are encouraged by their professional and scholarly organizations to present themselves as "scientist-practitioners" so as to emphasize that their teachings and interventions are underwritten by hard scientific evidence. But is this really the case?

After receiving my Ph.D., I began a 45-year career as an academic and applied psychologist. Strongly committed to a scientific approach to psychology, I spent the next 18 years teaching, researching, and occasionally practicing educational and counseling psychology and psychotherapy. Although I studied psychology as an undergraduate in order to understand as much as I could about myself, others, and our lives, I now found myself focusing almost entirely on particular kinds of behavioral, cognitive, and affective processes, functions, capabilities, and deficits that are the standard objects of psychological theory, research, and practice. During this time, I was increasingly concerned about what I came to regard as scientific psychology's inability to speak directly, broadly, and deeply to us and our lives as persons. In part, this limitation is a consequence of the fact that psychological research focuses primarily on aggregated group results and does not treat persons as the socially sensitive, active agents that we are. Because it does not take persons seriously, psychology is more about the demographic tendencies of groups than it is about particular persons and their life experiences. But there is much more that needs to be said in this regard, and saying it in a way that is grounded experientially in my own life and career as a psychologist is the primary purpose of this memoir.

How could a form of psychology more focused on, and informative about, persons and our lives be articulated and enacted if not through the scientific methods of psychology? To understand the exact nature of this challenge and attempt to respond to it, by mid-career I began to read and study the theory and history of psychology, as well as a wide variety of relevant literature in what has been called (cf. Jolly, 2017) "life writing," which includes biographical, sociocultural, anthropological, ethnographic, and a wide variety of other ways of learning about, recording, and understanding the lives of persons (both individually and collectively). Life writing goes well beyond the quasi-scientific aims and methods of psychology and their goal of predicting and controlling human action and experience in ways that are thought to be amenable to the purposes of scientific and professional psychology.

In consequence, the later years of my career in psychology provided me with much of what I had desired as an undergraduate student but had found missing from my early career as a typical and conventional psychologist. This memoir concerns my transformation from a scientific, psychological "technician" to a student of and contributor to a psychology of persons, our lives, and the human condition writ large. It tells the story of my movement away from a scientifically based applied psychology—one that diminishes and ignores people and takes insufficient account of their life circumstances—to a more broadly based psychology focused directly on persons and lives as they are actually lived.

More than any other academic discipline, psychology influences the ways in which we experience and think about ourselves, others, and human life. For all its claims to be scientifically and professionally neutral, psychology inevitably holds up a profession-friendly mirror that many of us understand as reflective of who and what we are and might become. I eventually discovered that a satisfying and productive career in psychology should be animated by a clear concern for people, one that does justice to our full range of powers and capabilities. I actually think that most psychologists share this concern and interest. However, despite being well-intentioned and concerned for their students and clients, as a result of their education and training they mostly opt for methodological conventions and models that reduce and limit the powers of persons to those of nonhuman animals, machines, neural networks, or inner psychological entities of dubious ontological status, such as information processing modules and psychic structures. Persons, per se, certainly did not figure prominently in the early phases of my rather disjointed career as an applied and academic psychologist, but I like to think they came to dominate my mature career in psychology.

Most who have the audacity to write a professional autobiography or an autobiographical memoir such as this can legitimately claim to have made major and perhaps lasting contributions to their fields of interest and expertise. Such is not the case here. I have been fortunate to enjoy a successful and mostly rewarding career, first as an applied and later as a theoretical psychologist, but my work clearly falls short of the usual standards that warrant writing about one's career. Some of my motivation to do so, despite the obvious setback of general anonymity (or, at best, modest renown in a few more marginal areas of the discipline), is undoubtedly fueled by the common inclination of older people to revisit the lives they've lived. This can be done in thought and in private, but I find it far more instructive to research and write about things that I am curious about. And I am curious about many, and even puzzled by some, of the events and experiences that comprise my life in psychology. There are two other reasons (insofar as they are clear to me) for writing this memoir. Firstly, I have had a somewhat unique career that has allowed me to understand and adopt different perspectives about, and ways of doing, psychology. I have worked in different sub-disciplines of psychology that range from applied areas such as educational and counseling psychology (which are often located outside psychology departments) to even more specialized and less-attended areas such as the theory and history of psychology. In distinctive phases of my career, I have been committed to different traditions and practices of psychological inquiry, ranging across quantitative–qualitative, experimental–case study, nomothetic–idiographic, and paradigmatic–narrative divides.

Secondly, my journey through and within psychology is a story of gradual disenchantment with its conventional scientific methods. For me, however, such disenchantment did not spell the end of my interest in psychology. Instead, it eventually made room and provided a renewed enthusiasm for the discipline, reconsidered as a psychology of persons and their lives. I want to tell the story of this reconfiguration. It is my hope that my experience and knowledge of different areas and methods of psychology and my story of disenchantment and reconsideration will warrant and repay readers' attention. I understand my career story as a movement away from an over-emphasis on, and valuing of, conventional psychological science to the study of persons and their lives. I believe psychology must make such a shift if it is to fulfill its promise to help individuals and communities to flourish. This is the message I want to convey, and I think the best way to do so is to tell readers about my life in psychology as a means of explaining how and why I reached this conclusion.

In this first chapter, I introduce the reader to a number of critical concerns about the ability of conventional forms of psychological inquiry to warrant and support psychological treatments and interventions with individual persons in their everyday lives. However, before I do this, it is necessary to talk briefly about persons. After all, it is persons that psychology is supposed to be about. Therefore, it is necessary to think carefully about what persons are. Only when this is done is it possible to see why much conventional psychological inquiry does not speak directly to them.

Persons as Active Agents in Our Lives

Persons may be defined as embodied, self-interpreting, human agents with a distinctive sociocultural ontogeny and uniquely rational and moral concerns and capabilities. Although all persons are biophysical human beings, the concept of a person does not equate with the concept of a human being. In addition to all the marvels of the human body, we persons also display a range of capabilities that results from our evolution and development within the interpersonal, sociocultural contexts of our lives. As we mature and develop from infancy, we become agents with the ability to act or refrain from acting, who are able to use language, reason, and moral concern to cooperate with others and pursue individual and collective goals and projects. We have a first-person, autobiographical sense of our own identities and lives, self-consciousness, and a unique ability to self-ascribe through reason and with purpose, as well as an ability to incorporate descriptions and practices available in the social contexts of our life experiences with others into our individual personalities. Human beings are uniquely social animals. Our personhood, with its attendant capabilities and powers, arises from our interactivity within complex webs of familial, community, cultural, and moral commitments and relations.

As persons, we are ontologically distinct from other animals and machines. Things do not matter to machines in the way they matter to us. Machines or other objects do not find significance in or care about their lives, existence, and fates. Other animals display limited agency insofar as their actions have consequences. They make things happen. However, they are not members of language communities, embedded and engaged in discursive practices that evidence genuine moral and rational concern for themselves and others. They do not experience shame, dignity, and duty in the way these are experienced by language-wielding, socioculturally sensitive, self-reflective agents.

With human culture as the linchpin, the development of children's abilities to cooperate with each other takes a unique ontogenetic form. By the age of six, kids are able to operate not only as individual agents but also as collective agents with shared understanding, intentions, and socio-moral values. It is this coordinative dimension of human existence that enables cultural practices of teaching and learning that are unique to human sociocultural transmission and development. These coordinating practices accelerate and power the development of human beings as persons. They enable new forms "of cooperation with almost total interdependence among individuals" (Tomasello, 2019, p. 342) and the emergence of a shared intentionality that allows humans to act jointly within partnerships, groups, and larger sociocultural units to create new forms of sociality and culture. The unique sociocultural capabilities of persons to coordinate their purposes, plans, and projects are evidenced empirically by the facts and artifacts of human societies and cultures (e.g., urban planning and community life, communication technologies and infrastructures, libraries and other repositories containing records of lives and accomplishments—the list goes on and on). It is an overwhelming empirical fact that members of no other species, primate or non-primate, work together purposefully to establish and maintain such complex and powerfully influential sociocultural phenomena.

We live our lives with a strong sense of personal time and experience, first-person perspective, and reflective understanding. Our memories and purposes extend into our pasts and futures. We live with a biographical sense of our identity, goals, and plans. We monitor and judge our successes and failures. Our lives matter to us and we recognize similar concern in and for other persons (cf. Taylor, 1985). Persons are social psychological beings. We attempt to understand our own and others' motives, actions, emotions, desires, and life experiences. All human languages are inherently psychological in that they enable persons in their various historical times and sociocultural settings to understand their own and others' life experiences and coordinate actions. As self-conscious, social, and psychological beings, persons are immersed in their life stories and in the lives of others.

The Limits of Scientific Psychology Concerning Persons in Our Life Contexts

With the foregoing understanding of persons in place, it is not difficult to understand why psychological research that involves persons as participants often fails to replicate. Recently, the Open Science Collaboration (2015) attempted to replicate 100 studies in cognitive and social psychology. Only 36% of the attempted replications succeeded. Since then, additional replication projects have cast further doubt on the scientific status of research in psychology. In contrast, any undergraduate student in a properly equipped physics laboratory can use equipment that sucks the air out of an enclosed tube containing a feather and a coin, invert the airless tube, and watch the feather and the coin descend at the same rate. This result does not vary across different locations, times, and experimenters. To the best of my knowledge, no such consistencies, equipment-aided or not, have ever been demonstrated in the applied areas of psychology, and few if any have been attained in basic research in the discipline of psychology.

Understood as socioculturally embedded and constituted moral and rational agents, persons participating in psychological research are unlikely to respond uniformly. Consequently, there can be no universal answers to general questions such as what forms of psychotherapeutic intervention are most effective or what personality factors contribute to human flourishing. In my early career as an applied research psychologist, I was frequently struck by how many individuals in high-performing groups displayed results that moved in opposite directions to that of group averages. It is even possible, if some members of a group that performs well on average perform extremely well, for the majority of members in such a group to perform below the average performance of those in groups that perform less well (cf. Lamiell, 2003). Why? Because persons who participate in such studies are active agents whose responses to experimental treatment conditions reflect differences in the sociocultural contexts of their lives and in the personal capabilities and dispositions that they have acquired through life-long interactivity in those contexts. As life contexts, lived experiences, and acquired personal capabilities and dispositions change, so too will the results of psychological research.

Results of research in psychology can also be affected by participants' knowledge of psychology itself. As Ken Gergen (1973) stated many years ago, "The dissemination of psychological knowledge modifies the patterns of behavior upon which the knowledge is based" (p. 309). Gergen's conclusion at that time was that "the continued attempt to build general laws of social behavior seems misdirected, and the associated belief that knowledge of social interaction can be accumulated in a manner similar to the natural sciences appears unjustified" (p. 316). Again, there is a reason for this, and that reason is persons themselves and their unique ontology. The idea of replicability as found and applied so successfully in some branches of natural science simply cannot hold for psychology, which studies persons who inhabit diverse sociocultural contexts and participate in diverse ways and forms of life.

Studying Persons in Their Life Contexts

The foregoing conceptualizations of persons and the implications of these conceptualizations for psychological research are drawn from the later years of my career in psychology. During the first part of my career as an applied psychologist, I tried to apply, despite some misgivings, the conventional scientific methods of psychology in my work and research. By mid-career, I was increasingly aware of the difficulties of doing so and the limitations that my use of such methods imposed on what I could study and how. I then attempted to develop more innovative and varied procedures and methods for capturing students', teachers', therapists', and clients' experiences of and learning from actual teaching and therapy—methods that were qualitative as well as quantitative and which were applied to individuals as well as groups. Only very late in my career and life did I realize something I perhaps ought to have understood much, much earlier: there is no need for applied psychologists to rely only on conventional empirical studies that restrict and manipulate persons and their life circumstances by forcing them to fit into psychologists' research practices and settings.

Much of the empirical evidence needed by applied psychology and psychologists is all around us, and can be observed systematically as it occurs in everyday life, or vicariously through careful study of relevant portions of the constant outpouring of books, documents, films, and other records of human experience and activity, past and present. Much of this is carefully organized in libraries, archives, and a wide variety of other private and public holdings, both actual and digital. Observations of human activity and study of its historical and contemporary documentation are always available to anyone who wishes to study the individual and collective life experiences of persons within particular temporal and sociocultural contexts and within and across the vast array of human experience and activity. In addition to doing whatever we can to improve our existing research practices by making them less restrictive and reductive, psychologists can also avail of this enormous empirical treasure trove of "life writing" (cf. Jolly, 2017). We psychologists can do much more in the way of everyday ethnographic and historical, archival research to supplement our existing methods of study. As Sigmund Koch (1999, p. 416) repeatedly said, "Psychologists must finally accept the circumstance that extensive and important sectors of psychological study require modes of inquiry rather more like those of the humanities than the sciences" (also see Martin, 2020a).

For example, why should applied social psychologists privilege empirical evidence from laboratory-simulated studies of evil, such as Stanley Milgram's (1974) studies of obedience to authority, over historical documentation, films, and survivors' accounts of horrific events like the Holocaust, material that is readily available in libraries, museums, and—increasingly—online? Do we really learn more about human evil from the empirical studies of psychologists than we do from studying the human historical record of evil-doing? If the usual empirical methods and accomplishments of applied and social psychologists fall well short of the standards of physical science, are they really superior to historical, archival, ethnographic, observational, and other methods widely employed in other areas of social science and humanities scholarship?

The plain fact is that applied psychology is not an applied science in the natural science sense. As Koch (1999) and others have suggested, it is time to recognize this truth and turn to the serious, complex, and detailed study of the lives of persons as actually lived—not for veridical statements of how things are with all persons, and certainly not as fail-safe prescriptions for living good lives, but as demonstrations of real-life possibilities that we might understand better and perhaps emulate, reject, or adapt to our own characters and circumstances (cf. Martin, 2020a, 2020b).

Having said all this, I do not mean to say that there is no use for traditional and conventional research in psychology and applied psychology. I think there can be a modest role for such research if it avoids overly general claims, clearly recognizes its limitations, and is focused on extending and deepening our understanding of persons, their capabilities (especially their individual and collective agency), and their lives. However, laboratory and survey research should not exhaust empirical inquiry in applied psychology. They must be considered alongside and coordinated with other modes of inquiry currently more familiar to those in the humanities and some other social sciences, like anthropology and cultural studies (e.g., Sugarman & Martin, 2020). Many forms of serious and focused inquiry into the nature, lives, contexts, and conditions of persons can demonstrate empirical and theoretical possibilities for human life and flourishing that a psychology of persons can consider and potentially incorporate. Much more will be said about, and illustrations provided of, methods of "life writing" in the final two chapters of this memoir.

The Story Told in This Memoir

The immediately preceding conceptualization of persons, assessment of psychological research, and suggestion for broadening psychological methods are drawn from my mature career in psychology. I include them here so that the reader can keep them in mind when digesting the chapters that follow. This memoir is the story of how I arrived at these conclusions. It is the story of my growing disenchantment with and subsequent attempts to overcome the reductionism and methodological narrowness that I believe currently makes it almost impossible for psychology to speak directly and meaningfully to us about our existence and lives as persons, and to help us to understand and navigate the obstacles and challenges we encounter in our lives.

From birth to death, we are caught up in a co-constitutive dance with others like, and different from, us. This is an ongoing, all-encompassing but loosely coordinated interactivity within which we get to know others and ourselves, experience and entertain different perspectives, and emerge as persons with agency and purpose. By participating as active agents in the communal practices and contexts that help to constitute us as persons, we inevitably make our own contributions. All persons are simultaneously culture carriers, curators, and creators. Dan McAdams (2013) has described the ontogenetic trajectory of personhood as one in which each of us moves through the roles of socio-psychological actor to agent and eventually to that of author, with some inevitable overlapping. I suppose this memoir means that I am in my author phase, but as you will see, my road to championing the psychology of personhood has been long and winding, littered with false starts and dead ends. Just how long, winding, and littered can be glimpsed from reading the last two sentences of my Ph.D. thesis (Martin, 1973), written by the committed behaviorist I was at that time:

The present thesis has pointed to the operation of causal connections in the production, maintenance, and control of human verbal behavior. The hypotheses put forth by B. F. Skinner, along with his more general principles and laws of reinforcement have been shown, for the most part, to be valid and to have great promise for the disciplined scientific study of human verbal performance.

(p. 141)

How I went from the person who wrote those lines to the one who wrote the previous paragraphs about persons as irreducibly active agents, applied psychological research as unable to produce laws governing persons, and alternative ways of studying persons and their actions is the story of this memoir.

An Overview of What Follows

In the next chapter ("Early Life and Education: Becoming a Psychologist"), I briefly discuss my early life, focusing mostly on my years at the University of Alberta, where I received my bachelor's, master's, and doctoral degrees. I also describe some of my experiences as an institutional attendant at a large Alberta psychiatric hospital and the influence they exerted on my interest in psychology as a possible source of help for both myself and some of those I met during the summers I worked there. However, the majority of the first chapter is devoted to describing my time as a graduate student immersed in scientific research and Skinnerian behaviorism, while simultaneously harboring some private doubts about such attachments.

In Chapter 3 ("My First Academic Appointment: Survival and Credibility"), I write about my first academic appointment as an assistant and then associate professor of educational and counseling psychology at Simon Fraser University in Greater Vancouver. I describe my struggles to fit into my new position and attain some degree of credibility teaching more experienced educators and professionals, while trying desperately to conduct and publish accounts of "well-conducted" research on teaching and counseling. Both were necessary if I was to receive tenure and promotion to associate professor, and thereby continue to help my wife support our growing family. In telling these stories, I provide concrete examples of research and related experiences that deepened my concerns about the empirically heavy scholarship in which I was engaged. Yet, despite such concerns, my success required adherence to the tenets and methods of conventional research practices in applied psychology and I was determined to succeed. A sabbatical year in Australia provided a welcome opportunity for me to revisit my fledgling career and make decisions about the future.

In Chapter 4 ("Academic Success and Personal Dissonance: My Theoretical Turn"), I recount the nine years I spent earning a full professorship and establishing a generally well-received program of research on counseling and psychotherapy at the University of Western Ontario (now renamed Western University) in London, Ontario. I discuss my and my colleagues' attempts to integrate a wide variety of research methods into our studies of the experiences of clients and counselors during psychotherapy, some of which were intended to recognize and treat participants in these studies as full-fledged "person agents." Ultimately, however (and despite the success with which our work met), I was increasingly discouraged about what I had come to regard as the false expectations and promises of conventional empirical research in applied psychology, even as I and my colleagues did our best to tweak and refine it. Given the pervasive individualism of most psychological theories and methods of inquiry, I was finding it deeply ironic that the scientific methods we were using, even with all the innovations we attempted, did not seem to speak directly to particular clients and their problems. Oftentimes, data from individual clients did not display the overall directions and kinds of change (or lack thereof) displayed by clients grouped together, and there were few journals willing to publish individual case studies, even if I might have been capable of crafting them at the time. By the end of my stint at Western, I had begun to turn increasingly to theoretical investigations of psychotherapeutic change and to theoretical and historical writings and studies related to psychology more generally. Perhaps such study would help me understand better my dissatisfactions with, concerns about, and increasing feelings of disconnection from the empirical work I had been conducting.

Chapter 5 sees me back at Simon Fraser University ("Finding a Home: In Full Pursuit of Persons"), where after a few years in university administration, I eventually moved to a full-time position in the Department of Psychology. There, as the recipient of a university-endowed professorship, I was able to pursue (in both my teaching and scholarly work) the kind of study in the theory and history of psychology that genuinely interested me. With some close colleagues and friends, I devoted myself to "theorizing the person." With Jeff Sugarman and others, I wrote, edited, and published books, articles, and chapters on selfhood, moral and rational agency, personhood, perspective taking, and related matters. During this time, I also rediscovered and developed further interests in biography, psychobiography, life writing, and the humanities that I pursued as pathways into a richer understanding of persons and their lives. In refocusing my career, I was helped greatly by many members of the Society of Theoretical and Philosophical Psychology, the International Society for Theoretical Psychology, and the Western Canadian Theoretical Psychologists, whose support, encouragement, and assistance are impossible to repay. For the first time in my life as a psychologist I felt truly at home, even if it was a home distant from the one I had initially envisioned as a neophyte, conventionally-scientific psychologist.

I use Chapter 6 ("In Retrospect: Reaching for a Psychology of Persons") to revisit the various shifts, changes, and themes described in the memoir thus far. In particular, I further elaborate on what I think is at fault with so much empirical research in psychology, including the ways in which it almost always succeeds in ignoring or reducing the personhood of research participants, even when attempting to safeguard their rights and provide them with instructive and helpful experiences. I also discuss in greater depth what I believe to be important advantages that attach to various methods of theoretical, historical, and biographical work in psychology and the humanities.

Throughout this memoir, I discuss and provide examples and illustrations of the influential and important ways in which professional associations and friendships, academic publishers, university administrators, and granting agencies fit into and help constitute the lives and development of academic psychologists. In doing so, I emphasize the overall importance I have come to attach to life with others within the various communities that help to make us who we are and within which our projects arise and take shape. It is at this nexus that my search for persons begins and ends, and where a psychology of persons and their lives melds with life itself.

References

Gergen, K. (1973). Social psychology as history. *Journal of Personality and Social Psychology, 26*(2), 309–320.

Jolly, M. (2017). *Encyclopedia of life writing: Autobiographical and biographical forms.* London: Routledge.

Koch, S. (1999). *Psychology in human context: Essays in dissidence and reconstruction* (D. Finkleman & F. Kessel, Eds.). Chicago, IL: The University of Chicago Press.

Lamiell, J. (2003). *Beyond individual and group differences: Human individuality, scientific psychology, and William Stern's critical personalism.* Thousand Oaks: CA: Sage.

Martin, J. (1973). *A functional analysis of verbal behavior in small learning groups* [Doctoral thesis]. Edmonton, AB: The University of Alberta.

Martin, J. (2020a). Methods of life writing for a psychology of persons. In J. Sugarman & J. Martin (Eds.), *A humanities approach to the psychology of personhood* (pp. 49–64). New York: Routledge.

Martin, J. (2020b). A proposal for a psychology of persons and their lives. *Review of General Psychology, 24*, 110–117.

McAdams, D. P. (2013). The psychological self as actor, agent, and author. *Perspectives on Psychological Science, 8*(3), 272–295.

Milgram, S. (1974). *Obedience to authority.* New York: Harper & Row.

Open Science Collaboration. (2015). PSYCHOLOGY. Estimating the reproducibility of psychological science. *Science, 349*(6251), aac4716.

Sugarman, J., & Martin, J. (Eds.). (2020). *A humanities approach to the psychology of personhood.* New York: Routledge.

Taylor, C. (1985). The person. In M. Carrithers, S. Collins, & S. Lukes (Eds.), *The category of the person: Anthropology, philosophy, history* (pp. 257–281). Cambridge: Cambridge University Press.

Tomasello, M. (2019). *Becoming human: A theory of ontogeny.* Cambridge, MA: Harvard University Press.

2 Early Life and Education
Questions and Ambivalences

I was born in the middle of the night of October 18, 1950 in the small town of Ponoka, Alberta, with a population of about 3,000 people. I was an only child whose father was a baker and alcoholic, and whose mother was a teacher who eventually became one of the first female superintendents of schools in the Province of Alberta. My mother was a talented mathematician whose father did not think mathematics was an appropriate career choice for a young woman, so she devoted the rest of her life to the education of others. My parents had been very much in love prior to my dad's service as an infantryman and sniper during the Second World War. But the drinking problem he acquired while overseas worsened when he returned home and tried to adjust to civilian life. He was my primary caregiver because of my mother's addiction to her career and long days of work. The silver lining was that my extended family of uncles, aunts, and cousins was tremendously supportive and knew how to enjoy life.

I was good in and at school, played most sports, took piano lessons, and had friends with whom I spent a great deal of time. With an October birthday and having taken grades four and five in a single year, I was younger than my classmates throughout junior and senior high school. Fortunately, my academic and athletic success, and the social facility I developed in noting and reacting to the subtle nuances of my father's moods, kept me on a mostly amiable footing with other students. A fortunate choice of close friends further ensured that I fit into those areas of school life I fancied. I was class president and valedictorian of my high school graduating class.

There was never any doubt about what I would do after high school or where I would do it. Not going to university was an option that never occurred to my parents or me. Both my mother and her youngest brother had gone to the University of Alberta in Edmonton, so I would too. To clinch a deal that didn't need clinching, my maternal grandparents had retired to Edmonton and would be available if I needed them.

Undergraduate Studies at the University of Alberta

In the fall of 1967, I entered the University of Alberta (U of A) as a student in its Honours Physics Program, where I struggled greatly because I had no previous exposure to calculus, something all my big city classmates had already studied. The time I spent playing recreational sports and varsity volleyball did nothing to improve my calculus. Nonetheless, I eventually managed to pass all my courses by the end of my freshman year. Yet, I did not feel confident about my ability to continue in physics. In fact, my first year of university was a jarring experience. I was unaccustomed to the anonymity of a large university and urban environment. Somewhat bewildered by the unwelcome novelty of academic and personal struggles, I overcompensated by excessive partying. I barely managed to salvage a pass in my various courses by immersing myself in a month-long period of intensive study prior to sitting year-end examinations. I can still recall the relief I felt as I opened the envelope containing my examination results—outcomes that were uniformly mediocre yet, amazingly, within university standards of passable.

The only first-year course I recall fondly was the required breadth course in English Language and Literature. All my other courses were in physics or mathematics. Although neither of my parents were keen readers, I was—perhaps a consequence of being an only child. Consequently, I already had read some of the poetry, short stories, and novels we studied and discussed. It probably also helped that I had a crush on the young professor who taught the course. She had an abundance of knowledge and interest in what she was teaching. Whenever I entered her classroom, I felt a sense of genuine enjoyment that was unique in my freshman classroom experience, or for that matter in much of my first-year experience in general.

When I enrolled in my first psychology course during my second year, it was a revelation to me. I was stunned at how much I enjoyed it and how easy I found it, especially when some of my physics classmates, who also took the course, struggled to do well. The instructor in Psychology 202: Introduction to General Psychology was Dr. Hinton Bradbury, a highly entertaining, engaging, eloquent, and knowledgeable junior professor. One of the many things I most admired and enjoyed about Bradbury's teaching was the way in which he was able to situate classic studies in psychology, such as Skinner's studies of reinforcement or Milgram's studies of obedience to authority, within the historical and social contexts of their occurrence. He helped us to understand not only what was done, but why it was done and why it continues to be considered important. Many years later, I often thought about and was guided by Bradbury's methods when teaching the theory and history of psychology to my own undergraduate students.

The summer after taking Bradbury's course, I worked at the Alberta Hospital, Ponoka, as an institutional attendant. Like most who begin work for the first time in mental health facilities, my initial experiences were ones of trepidation, amazement, and bewilderment. Nothing in Bradbury's course or in my previous visits to the hospital bakery with my father had prepared me for being on the wards and attempting to perform the various duties that had been assigned to me. Patients milled about in various stages of distress or sat rocking slowly, talking to themselves—seemingly locked in their inner workings. Every once in a while someone would yell out something, often incomprehensible, or pound a table in a sudden demonstration of upset.

Nursing staff circulated amongst all of this activity to conduct routine checks on patients' conditions and symptoms, update patient records, and ensure that medicines and other treatments were provided as needed. I and other attendants followed a daily schedule of waking patients and assisting them to get washed and dressed, or bathed when necessary, serving or taking them to the dining room for breakfast, readying individual patients or groups of patients for their stints in one or another center for occupational or other forms of therapy, and accompanying them to and from these venues. When not otherwise occupied, we attempted to talk to patients or engage them in some kind of game (mostly cards) or other activity (e.g., physical movement and exercise) until it was time for lunch, and on and on it went.

An overall effect of my experiences as an institutional attendant, in the summers of 1968 and 1969, was to increase my fascination with psychology. I was unsure if I ever wanted to work in such a setting again but I was completely certain that I wanted to learn more about why we behave as we do, for better and for worse. While going through the seemingly endless motions associated with the job of caring for individuals struggling with mental disorders, I was constantly trying to work out what was wrong with them and how they had become ill. In retrospect, I think my experiences with patients at the Ponoka Hospital contributed greatly to my later career interest in the psychology of personhood. How did patients experience their lives? In what ways were they like and different from me? Should they be treated as they were? How would I behave and what would I think if I were one of them?

At the end of my second year at the U of A, I changed my major from physics to psychology, overriding the protests of my parents, mostly those of my mother for whom psychology did not count as a "proper" scientific undertaking—a point of view with which I later was to grapple and mostly agree, at least compared to natural sciences like physics. That summer, I picked up a couple of additional courses in psychology by working night shifts at the Ponoka Hospital and commuting the 65 miles to classes at the U of A during the day. In the academic year that followed, I completed a degree in psychology. My third-year coursework was mostly in psychology, with some history and political philosophy.

I graduated with a BA (Psychology) with Distinction and received offers to pursue advanced studies from various Departments (Psychology, Political Science, Philosophy, and History) as well as an invitation to enter the School of Law. Because I was still playing varsity volleyball and I knew almost nothing about graduate studies, it never occurred to me to apply anywhere other than to the University of Alberta, where I eventually decided on a Master's program in Applied Social Psychology. This program was located in the Department of Educational Psychology in the U of A's Faculty of Education. The graduate programs offered by the Department of Psychology were mostly in comparative psychology and a version of theoretical psychology that did not interest me at the time.

Graduate Studies

From the autumn of 1970 to the end of 1973, I completed Master's and Doctoral degrees in educational and social psychology under the supervision of Dr. John McLeish, who had recently arrived at the University of Alberta from a previous position at Cambridge University. McLeish, a Scottish socialist, insisted that I read carefully the works of both Sigmund Freud and B. F. Skinner because of their very different commitments to social determinism. At the same time, through additional coursework in applied and counseling psychology, I was introduced to the work of Carl Rogers and other humanistic psychologists. The upshot was that when I graduated with my Ph.D. in 1973, I was intimately familiar with three of the major schools of psychology at the time—psychoanalysis, behaviorism, and humanism. Because McLeish had a great interest in social history and in Soviet psychology, I also became familiar with the history of psychology and certain branches of developmental psychology.

Like my mother, McLeish had a deep love for mathematics. In his later life, he published a book, *Number: The Story of Numbers and How They Shape Our Lives* (McLeish, 1991), which brought together his interests in social psychology, history, and mathematics. It was favorably reviewed in both the *Times Literary Supplement* and the *New York Times Review of Books*. Two of McLeish's pet peeves were that most North American psychologists were ignorant about the history of psychology and knew nothing about psychology outside the United States, opinions he embellished to include the consequence that "because of this ignorance they are able to view anything they do as significant and original." Like my mother's cold assessment of psychology as pseudoscience, this assertion was to stay with me.

My Master's thesis was a very routine study of relationships between academic achievement of high school students and neuroticism as measured by Cattell and Scheier's *Neuroticism Scale Questionnaire*. In discussing the results, I wrote that "the relationship between academic attainment and personality factors will obviously change with local social contexts and school selection" (Martin, 1972, p. 89), thereby suggesting that results from this sort of inquiry should be expected to fall far short of displaying universal effects such as those predicted by physical laws of mechanics, thermodynamics, and electromagnetism. Indeed, this first direct experience of conducting empirical study in psychology confirmed that psychology as a scientific discipline differed greatly from what I had learned and come to expect of science during my time as an undergraduate student in physics. Reporting results of statistical correlations between academic achievement and neuroticism as "measured" by psychologists' questionnaires was a far cry from using mathematics like calculus to pinpoint precisely the results of physical science experiments and predict future results.

McLeish agreed with much of what I said but argued that in principle it ought to be possible to study social processes and influences on human conduct by careful observation, recording, and analysis of behaviors of participants in well-established social situations such as classrooms or psychotherapy groups, which were "real world settings" of interest and were mostly constrained by broad rules of conduct and comportment. As it turned out, this was exactly what he and his two doctoral students were doing at the time. I recall thinking I'd be willing to bet a great deal that their program of research would not result in anything resembling formal mathematical statements of physical laws. Even then, I recognized the slipperiness of the "in principle" elocution. Nonetheless, I was interested in and wanted to learn more about what they were up to.

Noting my interest, McLeish and Wayne Matheson (a doctoral student working with McLeish) invited me to observe and learn more about their research on small group behavior in learning and psychotherapy groups. I never changed my mind about the stark differences I observed between what they were up to and what I and my physics classmates had done in attempting to confirm Newton's laws of motion in my first-year undergraduate physics laboratory class. However, I did find their research quite fascinating, and during my second and subsequent years as a graduate student in Applied Social Psychology, I became an active member of McLeish's research team. In my third year of graduate study and after completing my Master's degree, I was advanced to a doctoral stream. This was in the autumn of 1972, a year before McLeish, Wayne, and Jim Park (another doctoral student working with McLeish) published the results of their research, together with an accompanying theoretical formulation, in a book entitled *The Psychology of the Learning Group* (McLeish, Matheson, & Park, 1973) produced by the London publisher Hutchinson & Co., which 40 years earlier had published the first English language edition of Karl Popper's famous work, *The Logic of Scientific Discovery*. By then, on friendly terms with the three of them, especially McLeish and Wayne, I told them that their publisher was at least the same as that of a prominent philosopher of science, even if their methods likely would have worried him. Given the lack of distinction that had attended my brief time as an undergraduate student in physics, I don't know why I felt entitled to engage in this kind of science snobbery, but this is not the only time I recall doing so.

Because of the routine nature of my Master's thesis research and my ongoing involvement in McLeish's research group, I already had completed much of the work for my doctoral dissertation by the time I defended my Master's thesis. My Master's program had been filled with courses in social, personality, abnormal, statistical, counseling, and developmental psychology, as well as in the psychology of learning and individual differences. But there was no required coursework at all for my doctoral program, a project that grew out of the work McLeish had done with Wayne and Jim and out of a great deal of reading and talking he and I had undertaken to understand the then extant body of work on behavioral psychology—in particular the radical behaviorism of B. F. Skinner.

In my Ph.D. dissertation, I attempted a Skinnerian-based, functional analysis of the verbal and interactive behaviors of participants in an undergraduate seminar and two psychotherapy groups. My purpose was to test the extent to which sequences of group members' verbal and nonverbal communicative interactions could be analyzed in terms of B. F. Skinner's taxonomy of, and assertions about, human verbal behavior in his 1957 book *Verbal Behavior*. Unlike Skinner's earlier reports of the effects of reinforcement on the nonverbal behavior of laboratory rats and pigeons, his claims about the verbal behavior of human beings were not supported by experimental data. Although my doctoral research was not experimental, I conducted what I understood to be the first empirical test of Skinner's ideas concerning human verbal behavior.

To do so, I and a research assistant coded participants' in-group talk and gestures using a system I developed based on Skinner's 1957 book, and employed a computer program I created (with the generous assistance of Steve Hunka, Director of Computing and Research Services) to analyze sequences of coded interactivity among group members. To obtain the data analyzed by the computer program, the communicative behavior of participants in two psychotherapy group sessions and one undergraduate, small-group seminar were coded with the Verbal Operant Category System I developed based on Skinner's (1957) descriptions of different kinds of verbal operants and their functions. These numerical codes were the data entered into the computer program. The program produced cumulative occurrence graphs charting the frequencies with which each participant in the groups "emitted" each type of communicative behavior—i.e., Mands, Tacts, Echoics, Intraverbals, and Autoclitics, as defined by Skinner, and sub-categories of these primary types as determined by me. The program then (1) identified preceding and succeeding communicative acts of all group members during intervals of increased frequencies of occurrence for each type of communicative behavior for each participant, and (2) indicated which, if any, communicative behaviors emitted by any particular group member or members consistently preceded and followed each occurrence of the "target" communicative behavior. Whenever such consistencies were found, they were considered to indicate antecedent stimuli (if between preceding behaviors and the target behavior) and consequential reinforcements (if between following behaviors and the target behavior) for the occurrence of the target behavior.

In theory, the computer program was developed to respect the criterion that each and every occurrence of a particular behavior by a particular group member, during a period of increased frequency of occurrence of that target behavior, must be preceded and followed by at least one identifiable behavior of some particular group member (including the person emitting the target behavior, to allow for the possibility of self-prompting or self-reinforcement). Up to ten preceding or succeeding communication behaviors could be considered in the identification of possible "discriminative stimuli" and reinforcements. To count as an interval of increased frequency of occurrence, "the interval in question must contain at least three more emissions of the operant being studied than the previous interval" (Martin, 1973, p. 62). In my thesis, I referred to the selection of these and other criteria as "entirely arbitrary and pragmatic" (p. 62).

On the basis of the results obtained, I claimed that I had used the basic principles and concepts of operant conditioning that Skinner used to explain behavior in rigorously controlled experimental settings with non-human animals to account for human verbal behavior in the non-experimental group exchanges I had studied. "It can no longer be questioned that reinforcement principles and processes provide a powerful explanation for the behavior of human subjects in a naturalistic, non-manipulated environment" (Martin, 1973, p. 130). Even at the time, I realized this was overstating things. However, under McLeish's influence I had developed a bad habit of avoiding what he called "half measures." Nonetheless, I did not completely exonerate Skinner's claims about verbal behavior. I also noted that his experiments with non-human animals involved levels of manipulation and control that were impossible to achieve in the study of human verbal behavior in non-experimental conditions. Human beings displayed sophisticated and varied repertoires of verbal behavior that could not be parsed easily into patterns of behavioral stimuli, responses, and reinforcements. The very definitions of these Skinnerian processes depended on experimental manipulations and orchestrations that were absent in classroom and therapeutic settings. The computer program I developed to code my data used specific criteria to locate preceding and succeeding communicative behaviors for each target behavior during periods of increasing occurrence of the target behavior. However, these criteria were admittedly "arbitrary and pragmatic."

In re-examining my data some years later, I realized that one of these arbitrary decisions and another decision concerning the categories I used to code my data probably greatly increased the possibility of the computer program locating consistent sequences of communicative interactivity to support my Skinnerian hypotheses. The arbitrary decision was to consider up to ten preceding and ten following communicative acts as possible discriminative stimuli and reinforcements. The other decision was to add sub-categories of autoclitics (verbal behaviors that are based on or depend on other verbal behavior as stimuli) to my Verbal Operant Category System. These sub-categories included non-verbal behaviors such as "attentive listening posture" and "direct and continuing eye contact with the speaker" (Martin, 1973, p. 57). The combined effect of these two decisions likely greatly increased the chances that the computer program would locate consistent sequences of interactivity, which I then interpreted in terms of Skinnerian operant sequences of discriminative stimuli and reinforcement. After all, attending carefully to what a speaker says and maintaining contact with a speaker are not exactly unusual in group interactions. However, these did not account for all of the regularities identified by the computer program and that I interpreted as indicative of the operation of contingencies of reinforcement that controlled exchanges of verbal behavior in the groups I studied. Whether or not contingencies of reinforcement were better explanations of such recurrent patterns of verbal interactivity than rules and conventions of language use and social etiquette was a question that I would now immediately ask of such "findings" and their author, but nowhere are such questions entertained in my doctoral thesis.

Having described my methods and admitted that the conclusions I came to in my thesis were likely "overblown" and subject to alternative explanations, there are three features of my doctoral research about which I have no regrets. One was an insistence on conducting research in real-life settings (in actual psychotherapeutic and instructional contexts). Another was an attempt to report results for individual participants as well as or, as was the case in my doctoral research, in preference to aggregating data across individuals and reporting only group results. Finally, in the computer program I developed, whatever its faults, I was attempting to present data in ways that could be immediately grasped by those who viewed the printouts and the summaries and examples of them in my thesis. Like Skinner, I was and remain committed to the view that if something important is going on, it should be made as clear and obvious as possible. I know that I did not always live up to these three dictums in my subsequent career. For example, it was not always possible or reasonable to insist that graduate students whose research I supervised should be held to these three rules when the psychological research community itself seems to extol the virtues of complex statistical procedures and large sample sizes that almost entirely obscure what is going on at the level of individual participants in psychological research. There also were several times when I included individual results in research reports that editors of the journals in which the reports eventually appeared insisted be removed. These and related matters are ones I will allude to and develop further as this memoir unfolds.

Privately, I also worried that the verbal exchanges and sequences I studied in my doctoral research were not solely the function of what was going on in the immediacy of the small groups I studied. Much of what was said by participants in these groups went well beyond, and seemed very unlikely to be entirely controlled by, the immediate and concrete features of seminar or therapeutic situations. Indeed, there are many ways in which human beings differ from other animals, differences that make it extremely unlikely that, in the words uttered by influential behaviorist Edward C. Tolman in his 1938 presidential address to the American Psychological Association, "everything important in psychology ... can be investigated in essence through the continued experiential and theoretical analysis of the determiners of rat behavior" (p. 34). In fairness, Tolman added the qualifier "except such matters as involve society and words." However, given that humans are language using, social beings, it is extremely difficult to imagine what Tolman considered "everything important in psychology" to be. Nonetheless, other than one or two brief exceptions, which I have noted, none of the foregoing concerns were expressed explicitly in my dissertation. There, Skinner's behaviorism is mostly lauded and extolled.

I still think Skinner's approach to verbal behavior contains many interesting and useful ideas, but if the meaningfulness and intentionality of human interactions are to be captured in the overt verbal, vocalic, and nonverbal behavior of persons, more attention needs to be given to the historical, socioculturally established normativity of human interaction in ways that go well beyond Skinner's focus on immediately observable here-and-now exchanges. A more robust and extensive theoretical grounding is required— one that better captures the acquisition and use of human communicative behavior in the relevant historical, sociocultural, and ontogenetic trajectories and contexts associated with the emergence of relevant norms, conventions, rules, and everyday practices of language use. As it happened, in the years that closely followed my doctoral studies, I located much of what I found missing from Skinner's attempts to theorize human verbal behavior in the writings of Lev Vygotsky.

An unexpected benefit of producing and defending my Ph.D. thesis was to meet Ken MacCorquodale, a professor of psychology at the University of Minnesota. Ken was well known for his work with Paul Meehl on hypothetical constructs and intervening variables (MacCorquodale & Meehl, 1948) and his response to Noam Chomsky's famous criticisms of Skinner's *Verbal Behavior* (MacCorquodale, 1970). Ken served as the external examiner for my doctoral thesis. He was precise, eloquent, and genial in his questioning and criticisms, and greatly impressed those of us who attended a pre-defense dinner the evening before the examination itself. Fortunately for me, the oral examination went off without a hitch and Ken and I exchanged letters for several years thereafter, until his health began to fail in the early 1980s. The only annoying memory I have relating to Ken is the frequency with which my wife made reference to his good looks, style, and charm, and not just after the pre-defense dinner but for many years thereafter.

Post-Doctoral Years

Following my graduate studies, I was employed by McLeish and the University of Alberta as a Canada Council post-doctoral fellow for two years. During this time, I collected and analyzed data for McLeish and taught his courses while he enjoyed an extended sabbatical in Europe. To supplement my post-doc and sessional salary, I also worked in the U of A's Child Development Centre, which was devoted to treating and conducting research with families whose children displayed developmental and behavioral difficulties and delays. This was work that pointed to the possible effectiveness of a collaborative (between families and therapists) form of behavior modification for managing and encouraging nonaggressive interpersonal behavior. To encourage such modifications to be maintained in the daily lives of these families, we also used person-centered and humanistic forms of therapeutic and educational intervention that were tailored to the life experiences and situations of particular families and to the needs of individuals within those families. It was here that I learned a great deal from Dennis Brammer and Jane Silvius, who ran the Centre. They introduced me to a way of practicing psychology that was thoughtful, humane, and treated all clients of all ages with genuine concern and respect for them as persons. This might sound clichéd now, but at the time it was anything but.

My attachment to Skinner's ideas was also tested in classes I taught on "psychological theories of learning" and "the social psychology of education" during my two-year post-doc. I was becoming increasingly convinced that conditioning studies with non-human animals provided an impoverished basis for understanding the actions and experiences of people in ways that warranted intervening in their everyday lives. I began to add material in my lectures and class discussions that was informed by my experiences working in the Child Development Centre and the Ponoka Hospital—material focused on the complexity of human social situations and the obvious limitations of animal studies conducted in highly restricted laboratory settings as an adequate basis for human psychology.

During McLeish's absence, I got to know a few of the younger members of the faculty much better and benefitted from discussions with them during work and social hours. I found discussions with John W. Osborne of particular value. Osborne was an Australian-Canadian learning theorist who had served as a member of my doctoral committee and whose critical stance on behaviorism was considerably more advanced and sophisticated than my own incipient disquiet. Like me, he once had been a committed Skinnerian, so he understood exactly how to curb my unwarranted enthusiasm. Many of our discussions focused on Skinner's idea of behavioral self-control, understood as the application of principles and techniques of operant conditioning by persons in attempting to control and alter particular behaviors and life experiences of their own. I had tended to consider this idea as somehow legitimizing the behavior modification programs I witnessed and participated in as an institutional attendant and child development worker. I thought if an outcome of such interventions was that patients and clients learned how to control their own actions, such an outcome justified the psycho-educational use of behavior modification. Osborne would push me on this by asking exactly how experiments with rats in operant chambers ("Skinner boxes") were an adequate basis for intervening in the lives of other persons. By this time, I had become well versed in applied behavior analysis in clinical contexts with human clients (work that went well beyond Skinner's lab experiments and demonstrations) and how such methods could be tailored to particular clients and embedded in more eclectic and extended therapeutic programs. Osborne could appreciate that all of this might help improve things but kept reminding me to always imagine what it would be like to be a client receiving even the most humane-seeming behavior modification intervention. On many social evenings, he would sharpen and broaden this rejoinder by asking how my clinging to behaviorism as a scientific and clinical touchstone was consistent with the kind of freedom of expression and self-fulfillment I and many others seemed to be seeking in our own lives. Since this was the 1970s, Osborne and I both fit the somewhat pejorative characterization of "weekend hippies." Osborne kept reminding me that there is a huge difference between adopting behavioristic means of self-control and foisting such means on others.

Yet another John, the developmental psychologist John Mitchell, taught me much more about the work of Lev Vygotsky. Mitchell's interpretation of

Vygotsky's ideas promised much that I thought useful about Skinner's work on verbal behavior and did so with full recognition of the unique capabilities of human beings for moral and rational agency. Although grounded developmentally in verbal interactivity and linguistic exchange with others, Mitchell explained in detail how and why Vygotsky maintained that human thought and imagination could distance human actors from the constraints of their immediate situations and allow them partially to self-determine their actions. Somewhat ironically, I later learned that McLeish's major undertaking during his extended sabbatical from the University of Alberta during the latter part of 1973 and all of 1974 had been the completion of a book on Soviet psychology, which featured Vygotsky and other Russian psychologists. He too seemed to be increasingly skeptical and suspicious of our earlier enthusiasm for Skinnerian radical behaviorism.

Another of my post-doc experiences perhaps pointed to some of what eventually occurred in my future career. In 1966, Joseph Royce, then chair of the Department of Psychology at the U of A, founded the Centre for Advanced Study in Theoretical Psychology, for which he served as Director until 1979. On some Friday afternoons, I would walk across campus to the comfortable old house that lodged the Centre, to sit in on talks and discussions with guest speakers who represented some of the most well-known and theoretically inclined psychologists of the day (e.g., Hans Eysenck, Donald Campbell, Raymond Cattell, James Gibson, Sigmund Koch, and Rom Harré). I wish now that I had taken more advantage of this wonderful resource than I did at the time. Nonetheless, I was at least awakened to the fact that there were many voices, much more learned and sophisticated than mine, who shared and were able to articulate clearly good reasons for many of my suspicions of psychology's casting as a natural science, my growing concerns about the ethics of behavior modification, and the nature of us human beings and how we might be studied and understood. However, the seeds planted by those talks, if indeed they were planted, took considerable time to germinate.

While working for McLeish as a post-doc (mostly at a distance), teaching his classes in his absence, and working with Jane and Dennis at the Child Development Centre, I thought surprisingly little about the particular direction my career in psychology might take. However, as my post-doc appointment was drawing to a close, I realized something more permanent in the way of a job would be needed. In the spring of 1975, two professors from Simon Fraser University (SFU) in Greater Vancouver, Kieran Egan (later to become a well-known philosopher of education and educational innovator) and university administrator Ian Allen, visited the U of A for the purpose of recruiting full-time faculty members. I secured an interview and subsequently was invited to SFU to "give a job talk." Ken MacCorquodale, John McLeish, John Osborne, Jane Silvius, and Ted Aoki (a widely respected and innovative curriculum theorist who had also served on my doctoral thesis committee) were kind enough to supply letters of support on very short notice. The talk/ interview went well and the early spring weather in Vancouver, although rainy, certainly beat being surrounded by the remnants of a record-setting snowfall I had left behind in Edmonton. In July of 1975, my wife and I relocated to Burnaby, British Columbia, where I worked at SFU for the next eight years.

I met Wyn Roberts, or rather "re-met" her when, in my sophomore year, we passed in the main pedestrian thoroughfare connecting several large lecture theatres in the U of A's Physics V-Wing. In a hometown as small as Ponoka, everyone tended to know everyone else, and Wyn and I were no exceptions. As pre-adolescents, we had studied with the same piano teacher and had played duets in some central Alberta music festivals. However, we moved in different circles during adolescence, seldom attending the same parties or other social functions. So, I was not prepared for the effect our chance meeting had on me when we recognized each other in the V-Wing. Within a week, I contacted her, and we went on our first date to a movie, *The Lion in Winter*, at the Garneau Theatre near the University of Alberta. Three years later we were married in Ponoka and began our life together. Wyn graduated from the Faculty of Pharmacy at the U of A, and worked in a pharmacy on Whyte Avenue in Edmonton to support us while I completed my doctoral studies. However, she did not enjoy counting pills for a living and had little interest in becoming a businesswoman by buying into her own store. When I received the post-doc, Wyn returned to university to pick up some undergraduate credits in psychology that eventually allowed her to enroll in and complete a Master's program in the Department of Psychology at SFU.

Despite preparing to move from Edmonton to Greater Vancouver in the late spring of 1975, I found time to write a rough draft of what I hoped would be my first published book. I gave it the working title of "The Human Condition," with apologies to Hannah Arendt, and planned to find another title if it were ever to be published. It never was and I never got around to polishing it, perhaps because it was clear to me that it and I were not yet up to something of this magnitude. The book draft was a peculiar combination of behaviorism, humanism, and existentialism, with a dab of psychoanalysis. In it, I tried to lay out what I now recognize as a theory of human ontogeny. I wanted to explain human experience and development from birth to death, but lacked many of the scholarly tools and a great deal of substantive expertise necessary to make a convincing go of it. As it turned out, I became so immersed in simply trying to survive in my new position at SFU that any thought of continuing work along such exalted lines would be long delayed. In fact, it was many years before my everyday life conditions were right to support more serious and sustained work focused on the conditions and processes that enable us to become the unique psychological beings that we are.

References

MacCorquodale, K. (1970). On Chomsky's review of Skinner's verbal behavior. *Journal of the Experimental Analysis of Behavior, 13*(1), 83–99.

MacCorquodale, K., & Meehl, P. E. (1948). On a distinction between hypothetical constructs and intervening variables. *Psychological Review, 55*(2), 95–107.

Martin, J. (1972). *Neuroticism and academic attainment* [Master's thesis]. Edmonton, AB: University of Alberta.

Martin, J. (1973). *A functional analysis of verbal behavior in small learning groups* [Doctoral thesis]. Edmonton, AB: University of Alberta.

McLeish, J. (1991). *Number: The history of numbers and how they shape our lives.* New York: Fawcett Columbine.

McLeish, J., Matheson, W., & Park, J. (1973). *The psychology of the learning group.* London: Hutchinson.

Skinner, B. F. (1957). *Verbal behavior.* New York: Appleton-Century-Crofts.

Tolman, E. C. (1938). The determiners of behavior at a choice point. *Psychological Review, 45*(1), 1–41.

3 My First Academic Appointment

Survival and Credibility

During what proved to be my "first stint" at Simon Fraser University, I taught in the Programs in Educational and Counselling Psychology in the Faculty of Education and carried out research on teaching and counseling effectiveness. I also experienced, with considerable surprise, how different the life of a university professor was from what I previously, as a graduate student, had imagined it to be. I was not prepared for the seemingly endless tasks and meetings related to curriculum, allocation of office and research space, funding, student admissions, research organization and permissions, grant preparation and writing, graduate student supervision, faculty colloquia, tenure and promotion decisions, writing letters of support for students and colleagues, reviewing for academic journals, and any number of other matters. All of this surprised me, but nothing disconcerted me as much as my pervasive sense of not being able to find my place (where I fit and felt comfortable) within all of this activity. Although I was tenured and promoted to the rank of Associate Professor during the eight years I spent at SFU the first time around, I was greatly disappointed not to find or feel any real sense of conviction or purpose in my work during this period of my life.

Trying to Fit In

The main difficulty was that I did not feel qualified to meet the practical demands of teaching in a professional program aimed at preparing teachers and counselors for work in K–12 schools. Yes, I had some brief experience of working with children and their families at the Child Development Centre during my post-doc at the University of Alberta. I also had worked as an institutional attendant at the large psychiatric hospital south of Edmonton in my hometown of Ponoka, Alberta, during summer breaks while I was completing my BA in psychology. However, I was not a schoolteacher or school counselor and had no interest in becoming one or the other. Consequently, I did not feel comfortable, and certainly was not confident in teaching student teachers how to become effective full-time teachers or in teaching experienced teachers how to become school counselors. I sometimes felt like a fraud masquerading as a professor who had something to say to students, many of whom were much more experienced educators than I was. I still occasionally have a recurrent dream of being about to enter a classroom, and when I begin to do so, turning and fleeing from a chorus of boos. There might be something vaguely Freudian about this dream, but there certainly is no doubt that it immediately puts me back at SFU in the fall of 1975.

To compensate for my lack of firsthand, practical experience, I mounted (sometimes with graduate students and other faculty) several research programs to examine the effectiveness of different approaches to teaching and counseling. I also, during the summer following my first academic year at SFU, completed a postdoctoral clinical internship in the Department of Psychology at the Cape Breton Hospital near Sydney, Nova Scotia, an undertaking that helped me to qualify to practice as a registered psychologist in the Province of British Columbia. Soon after returning to Burnaby from Cape Breton for the start of the 1975–1976 academic year, I began, with SFU colleague Ron Marx and my wife Wyn, a part-time private practice as an educational and counseling psychologist working with children and their families. Having thus augmented my experience in and relevance to teacher and counselor education, through relevant applied research and clinical training, I was able to establish a degree of comfort and success in teaching courses in educational research and counseling psychology that did not require or presume direct K–12 teaching experience. My "running away" dream became much less frequent.

Initial Research on Teaching and Counseling

With a teaching assignment I now could live with, I turned more of my attention to writing the articles I would need to publish to attain tenure and promotion to Associate Professor. Borrowing from the experience I had gained during my doctoral studies in using observational systems to categorize and record verbal and nonverbal communications, I developed and tested category observation instruments to record teacher-student interactions in classrooms (Martin, 1976, 1977). Interestingly, although I don't recall making a formal decision to move away from behaviorism as a general framework for my research, the empirical studies I conducted at SFU retained only the occasional methodological link to my Skinnerian days as a doctoral student at the U of A.

I also participated in and became involved in evaluating a university-wide program that prepared graduate students to work as teaching assistants (Martin et al., 1978; Marx et al., 1978). Finally, with a group of graduate students whose thesis research I supervised or who I hired to work as research assistants, I conducted a number of studies examining the effectiveness of various methods of teaching and counseling (e.g., Schonewille, Martin, & Winne, 1978). The fact that almost none of my new faculty colleagues had any commitments whatsoever to behaviorism and that many were stridently against it undoubtedly played a role in my gradual abandonment of behaviorism as a basis for my work. Nonetheless, I still included the analysis of behavior, behavioral theory, and behavior modification in the research and counseling courses I taught.

Moving away from behaviorism did not, however, mean moving away from a more general commitment to scientific applied psychology. Even so, I continued to notice, as I had in my Master's thesis research, the very different ways in which individual participants in my research reacted to psychoeducational interventions. In one study (Martin, 1979), I and my research assistant were puzzled by the very different responses high school students had to an experimental intervention we were studying that assumed asking students "higher-order questions" would help them to think and learn more deeply. Although higher-order questions did indeed increase student higher-order responses (statistically speaking), this certainly was not true for each and every student in the class. Moreover, higher-order questioning was also associated with more negative student attitudes toward the teacher. When we eventually got around to talking to individual students, we discovered that some students did not respond well to higher-order questions intended to increase their interest and enthusiasm because they assumed that the teacher was attempting to show them up, catch them out, or reprimand them. Others were confused and did not understand how they were supposed to respond. Still others didn't notice that anything different was going on.

In this and other studies, even when the teaching or counseling strategies we were studying showed a statistically significant increase in student achievement or client progress, such overall effects were not uniformly evident in the results for individual students who had been in the classes or groups to whom these strategies had been directed. Sometimes, almost as many students or clients failed to benefit from such interventions as those whose scores and responses improved. In fact, among those who did not experience any benefits were a troubling number whose scores and responses actually got worse. Clearly, as individuals, students or clients were reacting very differently to the instructional and therapeutic interventions we were studying.

As the interviews we conducted with students in the higher-order questioning study revealed, different students could respond in radically different ways to changes in classroom routines and teacher behavior. In my first-year physics lab experiments, it was possible to obtain uniform results in studies concerned with such things as the motion of physical objects. It also was possible to state quite precisely and clearly conditions under which such almost consistently uniform effects might occasionally vary. Such conditions typically were very few and almost always the result of novice experimenter inexperience and error or faulty equipment. Obviously, results from research in psychology and education did not conform to such uniformities. Even more troubling was the fact that differences in student or client responses to experimental interventions in much research in educational and counseling psychology was seldom discussed or even mentioned in the research articles that reported the overall results of these studies. Nonetheless, such variation across individuals, even within the exact same treatment conditions, occurred across all the studies of teaching and counseling effectiveness I conducted with colleagues and students during my early career at SFU. Yes, we obtained statistically significant effects that allowed us to conclude that on average students or clients performed better under, or benefitted more from, certain psycho-educational interventions than others. However, there always were some individuals in the groups that showed superior results on average for whom these interventions yielded no improvement or benefit— and some whose performance or condition actually worsened.

Many years later, I got to know Jim Lamiell, then Chair of Psychology at Georgetown University in Washington, D.C., who has written extensively about the inability of statistical methods and testing to predict how any particular individual will react to psychological or educational interventions. In 2019, Jim published a memoir entitled *Psychology's Misuse of Statistics and Persistent Dismissal of its Critics* that appeared in the *Palgrave Studies in the Theory and History of Psychology*, a series of books I edited for Palgrave-Macmillan Publishers. In this book, Jim recounts his experiences and frustrations in trying to help psychologists and others understand what statistics can and cannot do with respect to determining what does and does not work for particular individuals. As I had recognized as a first-year graduate student at the University of Alberta, psychologists' use of statistics is a far cry from physicists' use of calculus when it comes to using mathematics to make precise scientific predictions.

Jim's main point is that "what is true on average" is not necessarily true for any particular person. To know that 60% of individuals benefit from a particular psychological or educational approach does not mean that any particular individual has a 60% chance of benefitting from that approach. It makes no sense to interpret a result that is true for a particular sample or group as true for any particular member of that sample or group. For example, if 60% of American basketball fans believe that Michael Jordon was the greatest basketball player ever, this does not mean that there is a 60% chance that any particular American shares this belief. Some are forever with Jordon;

others are unwavering in their support of Lebron James or Kobe Bryant or someone else for this distinction. As individuals, there is a very small probability that any of these others will change their views. Gravity applies to the physical bodies of every one of us; picking a "GOAT" (Greatest of All Time) does not—nor do particular psychological findings concerning the actions, experiences, attitudes, preferences, and beliefs of persons.

However, not all of my concerns about empirical work in applied psychology in education and counseling during my early years at SFU were confined to statistical aggregation, testing, and reporting. Occasionally, I was surprised by what can only be described as abject carelessness in conducting and reporting research findings. In one such instance, Olwyn Irving (one of my Master's students) and I attempted to replicate empirical results from classroom investigations reported by influential educational researcher Jacob S. Kounin in his 1970 book *Discipline and Group Management in Classrooms*. A major finding from Kounin's studies, frequently cited and reportedly replicated by other well-known researchers of teaching, concerned what Kounin called "teacher withitness," measures of which were said to correlate consistently and positively with student attention to classroom work and activities and consistently and negatively with student inattention and misbehavior. When Olwyn and I attempted to derive withitness scores for the 15 teachers in our study from codings of their classroom behavior, we found a jarring, logical inconsistency between Kounin's definition of withitness and his method of calculating it.

Kounin considered teachers to be "withit" when they dealt with student inattention or misbehavior in a manner that was both "timely" and "on target." "Timely" meant dealing with misbehavior quickly after it occurred so that it would not spread to other pupils or increase in seriousness. "On target" meant that the teacher correctly identified the student who misbehaved or initiated the misbehavior and that the teacher's intervention was directed to that student. Kounin's method of calculating withitness was to divide the total number of teacher corrections of student behavior in a given class period (what he called "desists") by the number of these corrections that were delivered in a timely manner to the correct student. For example, if a teacher issued 15 desists in a particular class period and 5 of them were error free (i.e., timely and on target), a withitness score of 3 (15/5) would be recorded. Using this method to calculate withitness ensured that the greater the number of teacher-issued desists that were error free, the lower the overall withitness score would be. Obviously, such a scoring system would result in higher withitness scores for teachers who by Kounin's definition of withitness actually demonstrated less, not more, withitness.

I sent a copy of our results and research report to Jacob Kounin for comment. When, after a month, I received no response, Olwyn and I sent our report to Walter Doyle, editor of the prestigious *American Educational Research Journal*, where our article eventually appeared in early 1982. Following its publication, I received a letter from Jacob Kounin, apologizing for not responding to my earlier communication and saying that since the publication of our article he had received a number of inquiries from colleagues asking if what Irving and Martin said about his flawed method of calculating withitness was correct. He attached to this letter, which I received on September 26, 1982, a copy of another letter he had written to Meryl Englander at Indiana University in which he acknowledged his mistake: "They (Olwyn Irving and Jack Martin) are correct in calling my stated computation of Withitness 'erroneous.' It does reverse the results." He then added that "They also point out an agreement with my results—at least a trend towards agreement if they computed as I did," and ends with "Basically then, there is no contradiction in the findings."

I still shake my head when I review this correspondence. Kounin seems completely oblivious to the fact that many classroom teachers followed and continued to follow his advice about classroom management and discipline, which he claimed was based on solid scientific evidence. In his letter to Englander, copied to me, any possible self-recrimination about how he may have inadvertently and negatively affected the education of students seems to take a back seat to Kounin's overriding concern with his scientific legacy— "Basically then, there is no contradiction in the findings." To the best of my knowledge, Jacob Kounin never issued any kind of public acknowledgment or correction of his mistake and its possible consequences. Unfortunately, similar stories are not difficult to locate in the history of psychology and social science more broadly.

Sabbatical at Deakin University

Despite my growing disenchantment with the purported scientific practices of applied psychologists in education and psychotherapy, by the time I was considered for tenure and promotion I had managed to meet the criterion of around 20 published or nearly published articles, which was expected of junior professors who would be allowed to continue their careers at SFU. A few of these publications related to work I had conducted at the University of Alberta for my Master's and Ph.D. degrees, but most were reports of methodologies developed or research conducted at SFU. In the late spring of 1981, I was formally tenured and promoted. And, wonder of wonders, I was granted a sabbatical leave, which allowed Wyn, our young sons aged one and three, and me to spend a year in Australia, where I had been appointed to a one-year term as a visiting professor of psychology and education at Deakin University in Geelong, a coastal city west of Melbourne.

The year at Deakin provided a much-needed break from what had been a hectic pace at SFU. Freed from our usual entanglements, the four of us had ample opportunity to enjoy much more time together and explore the state of Victoria, its beaches, and its—to us—exotic plants, animals, and customs. The only requirements for my visiting professorship were to give an occasional lecture and to participate in the activities of a research group led by Professor John Smyth, who had sponsored my visit. Otherwise, my working hours were flexible and allowed me to reflect on my academic career and life to date. In the end, I managed to publish a few more articles based on data I had collected previously at SFU and on my work with John Smyth and his research team (e.g., Smyth, Henry, & Martin, 1982). I also had time to let a significant fact sink into my thinking about my career—I was never going to fit into a teacher training program no matter how much empirical research on teaching or counseling I conducted and published.

I greatly admired many of the teachers and teacher educators I had worked with at Simon Fraser and at Deakin. But I was not one of them. I had no personal experience of teaching in K–12 schools and I would always be on the outside looking in on those who did. Of course, I realized that there were quite a few people working in faculties of education who also did not have much or any actual K–12 classroom experience, yet had very successful and satisfying careers. I had hoped that by conducting research on teaching I would develop a kind of proxy expertise that would compensate for my lack of actual classroom experience. I also had the impression that at least some teachers and student teachers with whom I worked were happy to accept my research work as qualification for entry to their teachers' club. Even so, I did not feel that I shared their world.

For me, conducting research on teaching did not equate with the daily grind of preparing and delivering classroom lessons, caring about students, developing supportive teacher–child relationships, interacting with other teachers and parents, marking and grading student work, and all the other, never-ending tasks that K–12 teachers must perform. In my mind, there was no way that research on teaching captured or allowed me to claim expertise in any of these vital areas of teaching and the lives of teachers. I had enough vicarious understanding of my mother's constant toils to know and be grateful that her experiences would never be mine.

My growing disenchantment with research on teaching and my role as a teacher educator was further encouraged by the modest success of a line of critical review studies I had begun after settling into my daily routines at SFU. Although there was much purported enthusiasm for team research by the university administration at SFU, I was well aware that getting tenure there would require me to demonstrate some solo body of work, or at least the beginnings of such an independent program of inquiry. With this in mind,

I began to book one day off a week to read, study, and write about theory and research in neo-behavioral and social cognitive psychology that focused on the phenomenon of self-reinforcement (so, it would seem I had not entirely jettisoned my behavioral orientation after all). This work was clearly connected to my doctoral studies and thesis in that much work on self-reinforcement was derived from or related to Skinner's radical behaviorism and his writings about self-control more generally. Skinner often suggested that individuals could use behavioral analysis to study their own behavior with a view to modifying it.

The social cognitive part of my work on self-reinforcement was drawn primarily from my study of the writings of, and exchange of correspondence with, well-known social cognitive learning theorist Al Bandura at Stanford. Like me, Bandura was born and grew up in rural Alberta. I also was influenced by Carl Thoreson and Mike Mahoney, ex-students of Al's who were working on self-reinforcement and what eventually would become known as cognitive behavior modification and therapy. I resonated with their work, especially their 1974 book *Self-Control: Power to the Person*, because it promised a form of applied behavioral psychology seemingly consistent with the idea that human beings could harness the powers of cognitive behavioral psychology to become active and effective agents in their own lives. Both Carl and Al came to SFU at my invitation and gave talks and seminars about their work. In our discussions during their visits, I often revisited themes and arguments I had had with John Osborne at the U of A during my postdoctoral days.

My own work on self-reinforcement (SR) took the form of critical reviews of the then extant and relevant literature. In 1979, I published an extensive review of laboratory studies of SR (with both nonhuman and human subjects, although strictly speaking I thought SR in nonhuman animals was stretching things) in the *Journal of General Psychology*, followed by a 1980 lead article in the *Canadian Journal of Behavioural Science* that discussed methodological and theoretical issues related to the study of external versus self-reinforcement. I concluded the *CJBS* review by stating that "a final decision concerning the advisability of a bifurcated 'external-self' reinforcement theory must await the solution of the methodological and theoretical problems raised" (p. 123). In my own mind, I was setting the stage for a program of work I would conduct in the future that would demonstrate and support an explanation of important differences between being controlled and exercising control, and between the conditioning of nonhuman animals and the agency of human beings. In recently re-reading this review article, I believe I can see my "then self" anticipating the beginnings of a theoretical inquiry into persons as moral and rational agents, such as I conducted at SFU many years later.

During the Deakin sabbatical, Wyn and I co-authored a "how to" book entitled *Personal Development: Self-instruction for Personal Agency* (Martin & Martin, 1983), which eventually was produced by the small Canadian publisher Detselig in 1983. The word Detselig was derived from spelling the first and last names of Ted Giles backwards. Ted was an independent book publisher and professor in the Faculty of Education at the University of Calgary, to whom I will always owe a debt of gratitude for his willingness to publish my first two books. The other one was a textbook for teachers, *Models of Classroom Management*, which had been published two years earlier in 1981. This book turned out to be the best-selling book of my career and might have helped me finally fit better in SFU's teacher education program if other considerations had not intervened. Two subsequent editions of the book were published in 1993 and 2000, with the assistance of former students Jeff Sugarman and John McNamara.

Although I did not continue to work directly on self-control and personal agency upon returning to SFU and for many years thereafter, for reasons that will become obvious, the final three sentences in Wyn's and my somewhat pedantic and naive 1983 book also (just as did my 1980 article in *CJBS*) anticipated much of the work on agency, selfhood, and personhood that was to dominate my later years as a mature scholar:

> We have attempted to view self-instruction from broader interpersonal, social, and cultural perspectives, and to consider our responsibilities to others. ... Self-instruction for personal agency ... places particular emphasis not only on knowing one's self, but on knowing what one can become.
>
> (p. 195)

Back Home but Far from Settled

Back at SFU following my first sabbatical, I was ready to distance myself from teacher education per se. As things turned out, there also were other, unanticipated factors that weighed heavily on my wife and me upon our return to Greater Vancouver. In our absence, inflation had hit hard in Canada and when we renegotiated a mortgage on the home we had rented out during our absence, the best rate we could get was just shy of 20% annually. With another baby on the way, Wyn and I began to look about for less expensive and more agreeable options for our lives and work.

To bring in a bit more money, I agreed in the fall of 1982 to take on an administrative position in SFU's Faculty of Education as Director of Graduate Programs. The Faculty was non-departmentalized and organized programmatically rather than by areas of faculty expertise. While looking about for alternative life and work arrangements, I also decided to write a textbook in what turned out to be a futile attempt to make additional money in the event that we were unable to relocate and would be staying in Greater Vancouver. My book on classroom management had sold reasonably well, so why not take another stab at a book for teachers? Biting back the irony (or worse, the hypocrisy) of not feeling as if I had anything of value to say to teachers, I dived into the task during evenings and weekends. I made use of everything I had been able to learn about teaching during my time at SFU, especially the work I'd done with Ron Marx and John Ellis (a senior member of SFU's Faculty of Education) in mounting a university-wide course for teaching assistants.

My plan was to provide a blueprint for teachers to use in preparing classroom lessons, interacting with students in supportive yet challenging ways, and evaluating and grading student work, while simultaneously (here I borrowed from my work in the SFU Counselling Program) helping them to combat stress and anxiety they might experience as neophyte teachers (something of which I at least had some direct, personal experience). I didn't really think it was much of a book, but to my surprise and delight, I managed to get it published by a major textbook publisher, Allyn and Bacon. Unfortunately, I was right in my assessment of it, and the book failed to sell many copies and was soon remaindered. It didn't take a genius to know that a book entitled *Mastering Instruction* by a young, beginning university teacher with an erstwhile behavioristic bent would not be a hit. So much for my plan to make some quick and much needed cash.

I've never experienced a year quite like the academic year of 1982–1983. With an administrative post added to my only slightly reduced teaching and thesis supervision responsibilities, my private practice, and my new book project, I simply had too many balls in the air. By the time Wyn was about to deliver our third child, I felt like I was running on fumes. However, I knew that if we could just get through to the summer of 1983, things would change and hopefully for the better.

For, as luck would have it, when attending a conference in London, Ontario, just after returning to Canada from Australia, I ran into an acquaintance from my graduate days at the University of Alberta. Dong Yul Lee worked in the Counseling Psychology Program at the University of Western Ontario. I talked to Dong Yul about the challenges of living in the expensive city of Vancouver and working in the Faculty of Education at SFU. The upshot was that after our year of being "house broke" and frazzled in the Vancouver area, and with the addition of a newborn baby girl, Wyn and I moved our family of five to London, Ontario. By the time *Mastering Instruction* was actually for sale, Wyn and I were no longer house poor, having positioned ourselves to take advantage of London's much lower prices and cost of living.

References

Irving, O., & Martin, J. (1982). Withitness: The confusing variable. *American Educational Research Journal, 19*(2), 313–319.

Kounin, J. S. (1970). *Discipline and group management in classrooms.* New York: Holt, Rinehart and Winston.

Lamiell, J. (2019). *Psychology's misuse of statistics and consistent dismissal of its critics.* Cham, Switzerland: Palgrave Macmillan.

Mahoney, M. J., & Thoresen, C. E. (1974). *Self-control: Power to the person.* Belmont, CA: Brooks/Cole.

Martin, J. (1976). Developing category observation instruments for the analysis of classroom behavior. *Journal of Classroom Interaction, 12*, 5–16.

Martin, J. (1977). The development and use of classroom observation instruments. *Canadian Journal of Education, 2*(3), 43–54.

Martin, J. (1979). Effects of teacher higher-order questions on student process and product variables in a single-classroom study. *Journal of Educational Research, 72*(4), 183–187.

Martin, J. (1979). Laboratory studies of self-reinforcement phenomena. *Journal of General Psychology, 98*, 103–149.

Martin, J. (1980). External versus self-reinforcement: A review of methodological and theoretical issues. *Canadian Journal of Behavioural Science, 12*(2), 111–125.

Martin, J. (1981). *Models of classroom management.* Calgary, AB: Detselig. (Reprinted 1985, 1989. with new editions in 1993, co-authored with Jeff Sugarman, and 2000, co-authored with Jeff Sugarman and John McNamara).

Martin, J. (1983). *Mastering instruction.* Boston, MA: Allyn and Bacon.

Martin, J., & Martin, E. W. (1983). *The psychology of personal agency.* Calgary, AB: Detselig.

Martin, J., Marx, R. W., Hasell, J., & Ellis, J. F. (1978). Improving the instructional effectiveness of university teaching assistants: Report II. *Canadian Journal of Education, 3*(2), 13–26.

Marx, R. W., Martin, J., Ellis, J. F., & Hasell, J. (1978). Improving the instructional effectiveness of university teaching assistants: Report I. *Canadian Journal of Education, 3*(2), 1–13.

Schonewille, J., Martin, J., & Winne, P. H. (1978). A comparison of punishment and positive reinforcement group contingencies in the modification of inappropriate classroom behavior. *Canadian Journal of Education, 3*(3), 21–36.

Smyth, W. J., Henry, C., & Martin, J. (1982). Clinical supervision: Evidence of a viable strategy for teacher development. *The Australian Administrator, 3*(5), 1–4.

4 Academic Success and Personal Dissonance
My Theoretical Turn

At Western, free from any involvement in teacher education and university administration, I now was able to plan a more carefully considered program of ongoing research on counseling processes and outcomes—a program of work that for the next nine years was supported by my new colleagues, the university administration, and the Government of Canada's Social Sciences and Humanities Research Council. Unlike my first experience as a university professor at SFU, this time around I knew enough about how universities worked to set things up properly.

I also had close colleagues like Ted Hallberg, Al Slemon, and Anne Cummings (one of my first graduate students in the Department of Psychology at Western who later became a faculty member in the Department of Educational Psychology) who were happy to join me in the research program I had planned. Others, like former SFU colleague and friend Bryan Hiebert, Wyn, and several graduate students at Western, Simon Fraser, and the University of Calgary (where Bryan relocated during the 1980s) also joined our research team and collaborated on site or at a distance. During my previous years at SFU, Bryan and I had begun to work together on a book entitled *Instructional Counseling: A Method for Counselors* that eventually was completed and published in 1985. Some of the analyses of counselor and client interactions in this book were used to create several of the coding systems we used to recognize and categorize such interactions in our program of empirical studies of counseling and psychotherapy at Western.

Research on How Psychotherapy Works

I had been hired at Western to revive what once had been an active center for research on counseling and psychotherapy, one which had begun to wither as clinician-researchers like Jerry Stone and Lisa Tsoi Hoshmand left UWO and the University Hospital in London, Ontario for positions in the United States. Taking stock of my new situation and ensuring that I would be doing work about which I was genuinely enthusiastic and committed, I drew up a plan for a hopefully innovative program of research on counseling and psychotherapy that would focus on *how* therapy worked when it worked well.

I was not going to make the mistake I had made at SFU in doing my initial research on teaching and counseling effectiveness. I now understood that asking a question like what is the "best way" to teach or do psychotherapy was the wrong way to go. Such a question was far too general. There is no single answer to a question of this kind. Any plausible way of teaching or counseling will work well for some students and clients and not for others. Even methods that work well in an overall statistical sense do not work well for all recipients. Nothing works for everyone. The statistical sense of "a general effect" (i.e., what is true on average) does not equate with "general" in the sense that an intended effect of psychotherapy is evident for each and every individual who receives it. This time around I would not focus on "what works" but on "how counseling or psychotherapy works when it does." To accomplish this, I would need to design studies that allowed for a careful examination of individual results and cases as well as group comparisons between those receiving and those not receiving a particular counseling intervention.

I also wanted to do everything I could to ensure that the empirical work we conducted would capture therapeutic interactions as they occurred in actual counseling settings. I wanted to get as close to the "real thing" as possible and stay as far away as I could from simulated, invented, severely constrained or staged counseling scenarios. In doing so, I hoped to avoid the artificial reduction of real-life contexts to simplified, quasi-laboratory situations that have typified so much research in the interpersonal, social areas of psychology.

With the generous support of the University administration and the capable assistance of my new colleagues in the Counselling Psychology Program, I was able to acquire the use of several counseling rooms with attached observational cubicles from which audio-video recordings of therapy sessions could be made. With the permission of University counselors, counselor trainees, and their clients, Ted, Anne, Al, and I (sometimes with the assistance of Dong Yul Lee, Bryan Hiebert, and Max Uhlemann, Director of the UWO Counselling Centre, Wyn, and several graduate students) recorded counseling sessions, interviewed counselors and clients following recorded sessions, collected and organized tapes and other data, used quantitative and qualitative methods to analyze and interpret these data, and wrote and published numerous research reports and papers in good journals in counseling psychology and psychotherapy. In the process of doing all this empirical work, we also published methodological articles about a number of techniques and procedures we developed to collect and interpret our data, as well as articles and book chapters in which we outlined and elaborated a theory of psychotherapeutic change.

Among our methodological innovations were a method of "stimulated recall" to capture therapist and client thoughts and feelings during therapy sessions, short questionnaires to probe what counselors and clients thought to be significant or important events in therapy sessions, several taxonomies and systems of therapist and client speech acts to code the therapeutic interactions we observed and recorded, and a procedure for producing "conceptual maps" of these events and related themes.

What we actually did in our studies of psychotherapeutic processes was to record one-on-one therapy sessions that we then played back to participating clients and therapists. Immediately after each counseling session, one member of our research team would meet with the client. Another would meet with the therapist. During these meetings, we employed our method of "stimulated recall." The researcher would play the audio-video recording of the session and pause the tape at particular points according to a prearranged schedule or plan. The participating client or counselor could also ask that the tape be stopped whenever she or he wanted to make a comment about what was going on, especially if the participant thought something important was happening. Each time the recording was stopped, the participant was asked a brief series of questions that varied according to what was being investigated in each study. The exact procedures followed also varied depending on the purposes and foci of particular studies.

When recordings of therapy sessions had been viewed and commented on in their entirety, participants were asked to relax and free associate as to what had occurred in the therapy session. A researcher wrote each word or phrase uttered by a participant on a small Post-it note. When free association was completed, these Post-it notes were handed to the participating therapist or client, together with a large sheet of laminated Bristol board (a thin but sturdy cardboard) and a colored marker. The researcher asked the participant to place the Post-it stickers on the board, using proximity of placement and lines and circles drawn with the marker to indicate how the words and ideas recorded on the various notes were "connected and clustered in their thoughts." Tissues were available if participants wanted to erase and correct any of the markings they made on the Bristol boards. Finally, therapists and clients were asked to rate their satisfaction and other reactions to the therapy session overall as related to the concerns that had led them to seek therapeutic assistance and to their overall functioning and understanding of their life experiences.

We conducted 10 to 15 studies using these and related procedures. The exact number depends on whether or not a small number of "follow up" studies or subsequent studies that "mined" data from several "original" studies are counted. Typically, 12 to 18 therapeutic dyads contributed data from 4 to 16 sessions of counseling or psychotherapy in each study. Once again, the overall aim of our program of research on psychotherapeutic and counseling processes and outcomes was to provide an empirical base for interpreting how psychotherapy or counseling works when it is successful.

A primary purpose of one sequence of studies was to determine the extent to which clients and therapists understood each other's intentions, actions, and experiences and whether such shared understanding was associated with their judgments and ratings of therapeutic success, therapeutic alliance, and other process and outcome measures. Initially, we tried to locate such "congruence" in moment-to-moment segments of therapeutic discourse that participants had selected as worthy of commentary during post-session interviews. For example, using coding systems that we developed and applied to tapes of therapy sessions and to recordings of stimulated recall interviews, we (e.g., Martin, Martin, Meyer, & Slemon, 1986) coded small segments of therapeutic interaction and related therapist and client stimulated recall responses for congruence across sequences of "counselor intention, counselor behavior, client perception of counselor behavior, and client perception of counselor intention" (p. 119). However, we later realized that such detailed, microscopic congruence across short sequences of therapeutic interactivity was too "fine-grained." Therapists and clients have very different roles in the overall process of psychotherapy. The main job of therapists is to use their experience and understanding of psychotherapeutic theory, process, and technique to assist their clients to comprehend and cope more effectively with their concerns. To these ends, therapists, using a variety of therapeutic approaches (which we sometimes compared and contrasted), encouraged clients to describe in detail their life experiences and reactions related to their concerns and difficulties. In this context, the primary work of clients required a focus on their overall experiences and reactions. If clients focused in too much detail on their therapists' intentions, actions, and interventions on a moment-to-moment basis, they simultaneously could not focus on the experiences that had brought them to therapy in the first place and how their in-therapy interactions and discussions related to their extra-therapeutic lives.

Eventually, we found potentially useful empirical evidence for the convergence and agreement between clients and therapists we were seeking, not in their moment-to-moment exchanges during psychotherapy sessions, but in their overall agreement concerning the most important events that occurred during a particular session (e.g., Martin & Stelmaczonek, 1988). Where our unsuccessful search for small-gauge congruence across brief segments of therapeutic interaction assumed an impossibly mechanistic processing of therapeutic "bits and pieces," our more successful search for overall agreement about important or significant events linked such events to a narrative about salient therapeutic happenings that connected them to clients' primary therapeutic concerns, issues, and goals. Such agreement was a decent predictor of participant-judged therapeutic progress, success, and satisfaction, even though oftentimes therapists and clients cited different reasons for selecting particular events as important or significant. Of course, it might reasonably be argued that such a result should have been obvious to us without all the empirical work in which we had engaged. After all, it seems reasonable to assume that therapists and clients will work better together if they share an overall sense of what is important and significant in what they are attempting to accomplish together.

Clients and therapists identified exactly the same events as important in approximately a third of the therapy sessions we studied. The fact that these sessions were rated as highly satisfying and helpful by clients constituted a major finding in our attempt to understand how therapy worked when it worked well (Martin & Stelmaczonek, 1988). In a follow-up study (also reported by Martin & Stelmaczonek, 1988), the same clients (six months after their last therapy session) viewed brief one-minute recordings from the beginnings of videotapes of those therapy sessions from which they previously had identified important or significant events. At follow-up, clients recalled accurately 73% of the events they previously had identified as important (40% from the exact therapy sessions cued and 33% from sessions other than those cued). Based on these results, we began to theorize that part of the answer to our overall question concerning how therapy worked involved clients' appropriation of what they regarded as important or significant "therapeutic discourse" into their own "self-talk" or thinking so that it was available to them when navigating their everyday life challenges and struggles. Here, for the most part, we were careful to make clear that it was clients themselves (not their brains or internal mental mechanisms) who were doing the appropriating, "self-talking," and thinking.

In an attempt to determine what made client-identified important or significant events memorable, Karl Stelmaczonek and I (Martin & Stelmaczonek, 1988) also coded the verbal discourse between therapists and clients that occurred during memorable events and exchanges in psychotherapy. To this end, we compared events recalled as important by clients with "control" events drawn from the same therapy sessions. These control events were non-overlapping with and distinctive from, yet temporally proximate to, client-recalled important events. We coded the discourse from control and significant events using separate six-point rating scales for "depth of meaning," "elaboration of meaning through use of figurative language," "personalizing," "clarity," and "conclusion orientation." All these dimensions were extracted from the then extant literature in cognitive psychology concerning determinants of memorability. We described our interpretations of our findings in the following way:

> One finding that we think deserves particular comment is the discovery that certain categories of discourse analysis, drawn from the theoretical framework of cognitive information processing, correlated with client identification of counseling events as important. Theoretically, it is hardly surprising that deep (thinking that is interpretive, critical, and analytic), elaborative (thinking that uses vivid language, images, and metaphors), and conclusion-oriented (thinking that includes hypotheses or interpretations) processing of information tends to be correlated with salient client encoding (identification) and recall of counseling events. However, it must be remembered that the data source for the information processing dimensions that we coded was the publically observable, verbal dialogue between counselors and clients. ... Perhaps, to paraphrase Wittgenstein, the limits of human conceptualization really are to be found in the limits of human language. At any rate, it is not unreasonable to expect that the often highly subjective character of clients' social discourse during counseling may furnish at least a limited foundation for the empirical study of client thought and memory processes.
>
> Understanding how clients bridge the gap between their counseling and real-life experiences seems to us to be essential to an understanding of how counseling achieves long-term effects. If we can acquire such knowledge, we eventually may be able to understand what counselors can do to promote and foster such client "bridging."
>
> (p. 390)

As I now read these words, across a temporal distance of over 30 years since I wrote them, they strike me as an extremely odd mixture of cognitivist, psychological palaver interspersed with a sprinkling of a more discursive approach to our data and its interpretation. It now seems obvious to me that phrases such as "processing of information" and "salient client encoding" are completely unnecessary, and potentially misleading, additions to what otherwise might be read as a straightforward account of client–therapist discourse that seems to link therapeutic interactions and discussions to clients' everyday lives. But, of course, by the end of the 1980s, when the Martin and Stelmaczonek (1988) study was published, I was reading and becoming more familiar with the discursive psychology of Rom Harré (1984) and the hermeneutics of Charles Taylor (1985). I also had now read a full and well-translated version of Vygotsky's *Thought and Language*, which had finally become available in a proper English translation (by Alex Kozulin in 1986).

In an attempt to offer a possible demonstration of how some of our research on counseling and psychotherapeutic processes and outcomes might be directly relevant to the general practice of psychotherapy, in a later study (Martin, Cummings, & Hallberg, 1992) we asked therapists to construct and introduce metaphors and use vivid metaphoric language to increase the likelihood that clients would attend to and recall important conversational events and insights that therapists wanted them to remember. As already discussed, we previously had found that psychotherapy tended to be rated as more successful by therapists and clients if they agreed about important events that occurred during therapy sessions. Moreover, both clients and counselors tended to recall as significant verbal exchanges using vivid, metaphoric, and distinctive language. If we asked therapists to use such language purposefully during psychotherapy at times when they thought really important therapeutic work was underway, would clients be more likely to recall therapeutic experiences at these times than when such language was not employed? We decided to see if we could conduct a demonstration of such a therapeutic possibility by asking therapists to intentionally develop and use metaphors during what they regarded as periods of "important therapeutic work" (Martin, Cummings, & Hallberg, 1992). By this time, I had come to regard psychological research as providing demonstrations of perhaps useful possibilities with respect to the phenomena being investigated, not as yielding anything close to definitive scientific tests of hypotheses that might yield generalizable, let alone definitive, conclusions.

As a "sidebar," I've often reflected on the fact that many of the most well-known and influential research studies in the history of psychology (e.g., Ebbinghaus' studies of his own memory, Watson and Rayner's aversive conditioning of Little Albert, Milgram's studies of obedience to authority, Zimbardo's Stanford prison study, etc.) were not experiments per se and certainly would not rate highly as providing "evidence" under the rules and conventions of contemporary "best practice" guidelines adopted and promoted by most psychological associations. Would not these classic works be described more accurately as demonstrations, or perhaps even performances?

Getting back to the Martin et al. (1992) study of therapists' intentional use of metaphor, four person-centered, experiential therapists were asked to plan and use at least one appropriate metaphor (conveyed with vivid language) in each of 41 therapy sessions drawn from their regular caseloads. Immediately after the completion of each session, clients were interviewed by members of our research team. During these post-session interviews, each client was asked to review the just-completed therapy session by recalling "exact words, phrases, or sentences spoken during the session." Each client then was asked to respond as specifically as possible to the following questions: "What was the most memorable event that occurred in this session?" and "Why do you remember this event?" The post-session interviews continued by repeatedly asking clients to recall the next most memorable event until any events the clients considered to be especially memorable were covered. At the end of the interviews, clients were asked to rate the helpfulness of the session on a five-point scale, ranging from "not at all helpful" to "extremely helpful." Therapists were also interviewed after each session and asked which metaphors they had intentionally used and elaborated.

A client was considered to have recalled a therapist's intentional use of metaphor in a particular session if the client's recollection contained some of the same words and phrases used by the therapist to introduce and develop the metaphor and to capture its gist. Overall, clients recalled therapists' intentional use of metaphor in specific detail for 66% of the occasions on which therapists reported intentionally using metaphoric language to highlight what they considered to be therapeutically important occurrences and content during psychotherapy. In other words, two-thirds of therapists' attempts to initiate and engage clients through the use of metaphor and metaphoric language were recalled by clients to whom these attempts were directed. Discourse analysis of the recordings of the actual therapy sessions indicated that in 95% of "metaphoric events" intended by therapists and actually recalled by clients, the metaphoric language initiated by therapists was "picked up and used explicitly by clients." Sessions in which clients collaborated with therapists in developing therapeutic metaphors introduced intentionally by therapists were also rated as much more helpful than other sessions (Martin, Cummings, & Hallberg, 1992). Post-session interviews indicated that clients believed the use and development of metaphors in therapy enhanced their emotional awareness and understanding by making affective, experiential content more accessible, enhanced their relationships with their therapists, and helped to clarify their personal goals for therapy.

The cognitivism that dominated psychology during the 1980s was also apparent in another stream of studies in our overall program of research on how counseling and psychotherapy work. Here, we attempted to explore possible differences that might exist between how novice and more experienced therapists conceptualized their clients and the therapeutic process. In one such study (Martin, Slemon, Hiebert, Hallberg, & Cummings, 1989), we used the "conceptual mapping" "Bristol board" procedure, described earlier, to examine conceptualizations of 23 (11 experienced versus 12 novice) counselors concerning general counseling process and specific client concerns. Previous studies in this general area of inquiry had used standardized questionnaires to probe therapist conceptualizations that were unrelated to any particular therapeutic interventions with specific clients. Consistent with our entire program of research on counseling, our overall intention was to conduct our studies in ways that heightened their external validity and likely relationship to counseling and therapy as conducted in non-research settings.

Multivariate analysis of variance of our data revealed an interaction effect of therapist experience (experienced versus novice) with generality of conceptual task (general counseling focus versus case specific focus) on the extensiveness of counselor conceptualizations. Experienced counselors displayed more extensive conceptualizations on a Bristol board mapping task that focused on general counseling process and less extensive conceptualizations on a Bristol board mapping task that focused on the specific session completed just prior to the administration of these tasks. Order of completion of the two Bristol board tasks, with either a general or a specific focus, was counterbalanced across and within successive completion of these tasks by participating counselors, in an attempt to control for sequence effects such as fatigue or boredom with the research procedures. Our interpretation of these findings was that "experienced counselors possess extensive abstract, general knowledge of counseling that they use to conceptualize specific instances of counseling efficiently ad parsimoniously" whereas "novice counselors, who lack such abstracted knowledge, engage in more extensive, seemingly unique conceptual work for each separate client" (Martin, et al., 1989, p. 395). In our discussion, we concluded by saying:

> In domains such as mathematics, experience … is more readily correlated with expertise. In areas such as counseling, where such correlations have not been established (or are much debated), it remains an open question as to whether or not phenomena like the preexistence of organized, abstract knowledge and an ensuing automatization of conceptualization processes actually facilitate or detract from effectiveness as a human service professional.

(p. 399)

Another study (Martin, Martin, & Slemon, 1989) returned to some of the more microscopic analyses of cognitive-behavioral therapeutic sequences we previously had found unhelpful when searching for forms of therapist–client coordination and congruence that might be associated with therapeutic effectiveness. In taking a second look at such sequences of interactivity, we were attempting a more theoretical inquiry into the possible regularity and use of particular patterns of interaction. Qualitative methods of sequential discourse analysis and quantitative methods of conditional probability calculations were used to provide "data on the probabilities of frequently occurring sequences of counselor intentions, counselor behaviors, client cognitive operations, and client responses … taken from 18 different counseling dyads," each of which contributed "data from 3 to 8 separate counseling sessions, selected at regular intervals across 10- to 16-session therapeutic interventions" (p. 8). As in my doctoral research at the University of Alberta (but this time without the Skinnerian behaviorism that guided that earlier work), the purpose was "to determine if there were distinctive patterns of actions and acts in counseling interactions that might provide a basis for a social science of counseling psychology" (p. 8). Our answer to this question was a resounding "maybe," to which we added a number of caveats. In particular, we were clear that we did not examine whether or not different approaches to counseling and therapy, differences in counselor experience and expertise, and more versus less effective therapeutic interventions might promote and contain different sequences of therapist–client interactivity.

Relating our results to the actual practice of counseling and psychotherapy, we concluded that:

> the skill, strategy, and intervention training that many students receive in their courses, practicums, and internships in counseling psychology may assume a tighter brand of action-act determinism than can be supported by a careful scrutiny of extant empirical results in this area. ... We may never succeed in developing an empirically based social science of counseling ... but we may eventually develop a clearer understanding of [some frequently occurring] patterns of counseling interaction.
> (Martin et al., 1989, p. 16)

In a subsequent theoretical article (Martin, 1990), I specifically mentioned that any such search for tight determinism across sequences of human interaction in psychotherapy or elsewhere must reckon with the ever-present possibility of the agentive capabilities of human participants in such interactions.

> Research on client reactions to therapeutic interventions and therapist behaviors indicates that individual differences are extensive and ubiquitous in counseling and psychotherapy ... In my view, the nature of human [action] does not yield to a tightly-deterministic account. Expectations for tight algorithms in any prescriptive science are unwarranted.
> (pp. 78–79)

As I look back on these various studies I conducted with others at UWO, I find myself somewhat torn between what I consider to be some of their merits and what I consider to be some of their limitations. I continue to believe that these studies are in many ways exemplary in their search for an empirically-supported and grounded understanding of the complexities of successful therapeutic interactions in actual therapeutic situations. However, our use of general ratings of therapeutic outcome and systems of coding therapeutic interactions were mostly free of specific content with respect to clients' particular concerns and difficulties. Nor did we consider differences in therapists' approaches to psychotherapy or in their therapeutic styles. We also failed to document the nature and extent of client problems and the extent or kind of social-emotional supports and resources available in their lives. Our designs and methodologies ignored these and other likely influential differences on client functioning by simply failing to take them into account. In addition, some of the cognitive theory and language we used to describe our studies and instruct clients to complete "stimulated recall" and "conceptual mapping" tasks may have led some participants to think of their problems and concerns as primarily caused by their own ways of thinking, over and above their ways of interacting with, and relating to, others in their lives.

Although our studies included both qualitative and quantitative data and methods, the conventions and formats governing acceptable reporting of research in applied psychology ensured that our inclusion of case examples in our research write-ups were eclipsed by (and sometimes removed from our reports to make more room for) the reporting of aggregate statistical data and tests. I must admit to being genuinely surprised, when re-reading and reconsidering the published articles reporting our research, by the amount of space in these reports devoted to detailing with great precision exactly what we did as researchers compared to the relative absence of elaboration concerning individual therapists and clients and their experiences. Equally prevalent was a tendency to pay scant attention to anomalies in our data compared to a general highlighting of commonalities. All these tendencies and conventions in the reporting of our studies and results clearly limit the extent to which the participants in our research appear as person agents, relegating them to the status of compliant subjects who conformed to our research procedures, instructions, and directions. Narratives of personal agency were excluded in favor of elaborated reporting of methodologies and technical procedures associated with data collection, recording, coding, and analysis. In short, we mostly ignored the agency of participants in our research and hid the extensive agency we exercised as researchers behind a barrage of methodological rigor.

Sabbatical at the University of Iowa and the Benefits of Travel

Based on my peers' and the University administration's evaluation of my research, teaching, and service at UWO, I was promoted to Full Professor in the Departments of Educational Psychology and Psychology in 1986. Soon thereafter, I was awarded a sabbatical leave for the 1987–1988 university year. In the late summer of 1987, Wyn, I, and our three children moved to Iowa City, Iowa, where I could interact with a small number of counseling psychologists and psychotherapists who were doing research related to my own and seemed happy to put up with me for a year.

Jerry Stone, who previously had been a professor of psychology at UWO and director of the UWO Counselling Centre, was now the director of the University of Iowa Counseling Services. He and others at the University of Iowa, like Charles Claiborn and Betsy Altmeier, made me very welcome and I learned a great deal from my interactions with all of them. I knew Jerry, Chuck, and Betsy from my attendance at annual meetings of the Counseling Psychology Division of the American Psychological Association, but having the opportunity of working more closely with them over an extended period of time was invaluable.

Without teaching and administrative commitments, I was free to enjoy many discussions about academic life, research in applied psychology, and psychology and social science more generally. In particular, I found it very useful to discuss my growing misgivings concerning the limitations I now sensed in conventional psychological theory and research and was trying to articulate. Chuck, Betsy, and Jerry did not necessarily agree with me but they were kind enough to hear me out and share their own views and life experiences. I recall discussions concerning tensions between conflicting demands and orientations of research versus professional practices as especially interesting and relevant.

During the mid to late 1980s, Iowa was not the only stop on my burgeoning travel agenda. In the early 1980s, I sent a copy of a research article (Haynes, Marx, Martin, Wallace, Merrick, & Einarson, 1983) to renowned psychotherapist Albert Ellis, which supported the effectiveness of Ellis' psychotherapeutic approach known as rational-emotive therapy (RET). At the time, Ellis dropped me a note saying that he greatly appreciated my sending him a copy of the article. Somewhat later, in the spring of 1985, he invited me to spend a weekend at his New York Rational-Emotive Institute, housed on the lower floors of his Upper Eastside Manhattan townhouse, which also contained his private residence on the top levels. So popular was Ellis' approach to group psychotherapy that on Friday evenings he opened a large ground-level room to anyone who wanted to "drop in" for a group therapy session with him as group leader.

In one of his letters to me, Ellis described his therapeutic approach: "The main theory of RET says that when humans rigidly take their preferences and escalate them into absolutistic musts they become emotionally disturbed." In the interactions I witnessed during my 1985 visit, Ellis repeatedly zeroed in on participants' comments in which he detected such escalations. For example, when group members became or reported themselves as emotionally upset by what they regarded as hurtful or dismissive comments or behaviors from others, he would ask them if they believed they must never be offended or hurt. Eventually, several such instances would cumulate to a point where Ellis would explain that it was irrational to insist that others never behave in hurtful ways and to get worked up unduly by such occurrences:

> By insisting that we must never be insulted or upset, we only increase the likelihood that we will feel insulted or upset. Once we put aside this irrational insistence, we can think more clearly about how to respond or if indeed a response is necessary at all.

Although Ellis clearly appreciated my formal empirical verification of the efficacy of his approach to psychotherapy, I noted in our conversations that weekend that he never made a point of emphasizing formal research and its findings over insights he had gleaned through many years of clinical practice. Instead of talking about the scientific foundations of his approach, he repeatedly talked about the grounding of his therapeutic theory and methods in reason and careful attention to his clients' illogical and self-defeating talk and actions in therapy and in their everyday lives. Time and again, he would remind me that science as practiced in psychological research was not the only, and certainly not the most important, empirical evidence on which to base therapeutic interventions and strategies. Evidence gathered by careful consideration of our everyday experience is what matters most to us, and what we use to guide our thoughts and actions. I came away with a much greater appreciation of what an attentive psychotherapist could learn about human beings (about persons and their lives) by a careful study of his own and others' words, actions, and life choices. Of course, such careful observation and "interpretation in context" are standard empirical methods in social sciences such as anthropology and ethnography.

Further afield, the summers immediately before and after my academic year at the University of Iowa offered international experiences that further confirmed my belief in the importance of social and cultural contexts as powerful sources of personhood. I spent much of July and August in 1987 and 1988 in Portugal at the invitation of Bartolo Campos, Director of Psychology at the University of Oporto, and Oscar Gonçalves, a young psychotherapist I had met during conferences organized by the Society for Psychotherapy Research. Bartolo and Oscar were committed to "internationalizing" Portuguese psychology programs during the 1980s. Jim Marcia, a clinical and developmental psychologist from the Department of Psychology at Simon Fraser University, and I were the Canadian members of a team of international psychologists selected as consultants and advisors to their efforts.

In Portugal I had a firsthand opportunity to study and talk about psychotherapeutic interactions in social and cultural contexts very different from those I was familiar with in Canada and the United States. As I had done during my time in Australia, I noted carefully the interpersonal and familial interactions and sociocultural customs and values that differed very noticeably from those with which I was familiar. No matter how much Oscar and Bartolo took from what we consultants had to say and suggest, it was clear to me that it would need to be adapted to their and their clients' own ways of life. Indeed, when I observed their work with clients and students, I saw them make, almost automatically, necessary changes and refinements to suit life in Portugal. Like the expressive melancholy of Portuguese fado, played and sung late at night over port with friends and family, the lives and life concerns of people must be experienced in their contexts of development and occurrence. Assuming the necessity of a healthy and functioning body, what matters most to us in life are our conventions, customs, values, beliefs, and aspirations—that is, our ways of understanding and living.

Gaining additional and more diverse perspectives on life possibilities is one of many benefits of the travel that attends a bit of academic success. Although I have now grown tired of extended travel and its inconveniences, during my 30s, 40s, and 50s, I loved the adventure and learning attained by immersing myself in other ways of being and knowing. And, of course, I enjoyed the recognition of my work by many of those who were gracious enough to host and otherwise make arrangements for my travels and participation in conferences, research centers, and other professional and scholarly activities.

On a lighter note, one of the more humorous travel incidents I experienced during this phase of my life as a psychologist was a trip to a specialized conference for computing scientists and psychotherapists in Namur, Belgium. Previously unbeknownst to me, this gathering turned out to be funded partly by the Central Intelligence Agency of the United States. The CIA wanted to improve computerized counseling programs (more sophisticated versions of early programs like ELIZA) that the Agency hoped could be used to offer therapeutic treatment to ex-members suffering from PTSD without running the risk of them sharing classified information with actual psychotherapists. I spent much of my conference time being wined and dined, feeling as if I were a character in a novel by David Lodge or Tom Sharpe. In the end, however, I declined further involvement with the conference organizers and their project.

Finishing Up and Moving On

As the 1980s ended, our research group at Western had become a prolific producer of published research in counseling and psychotherapy. We collected a number of national and international awards for our efforts. I personally was invited to be a fellow of both the Canadian and American Psychological Associations. My theoretical interpretation of our overall program of empirical work eventually appeared in *The Construction and Understanding of Psychotherapeutic Change: Conversations, Memories, and Theories* (Martin, 1994).

In this book and in a 1992 chapter I prepared for a volume edited by Shaké Toukmanian and my good friend David Rennie, *Psychotherapy Process Research*, I wrote about the research, methodological, and theoretical work of our Counselling Psychology research group at Western (Martin, 1992). In particular, I emphasized what we had learned and our ideas about how psychotherapy worked when it was successful. I was careful to avoid the difficulties of claiming to know what kinds of intervention would work best and to avoid other general claims about psychotherapeutic effectiveness. Instead, I described the yield from our nine years of collaborative research efforts in the following way:

> When individuals' current theories and the actions they support do not permit the attainment of desired personal goals, acceptable resolutions to personal problems/concerns, or acceptable levels of personal coping, they suffer emotional upset and often seek change. Psychotherapy is a unique form of social conversation and interpersonal activity that attempts to help individuals to alter their personal theories so as to permit more effective goal attainment, problem resolution, or personal coping. Psychotherapists work collaboratively with clients to elaborate their clients' current personal theories by facilitating memory-mediated recall, interpretation, and analysis of their past and current experiences and understandings in the therapeutic conversation. Therapists' purposeful use of certain discourse such as imagery, metaphor, and other concrete, affectively laden language may facilitate such memory-mediated elaboration of clients' theories. Psychotherapists also work collaboratively with clients to help them revise their theories once these have been elaborated. Such revision is achieved by clients' memory-mediated internalization of the therapeutic conversations and activities through which their theories have elaborated, interpreted, and analyzed. [This] is especially likely when content and understandings contained in the therapeutic conversations are perceived by clients as both *relevant* to, yet somehow *inconsistent* with, their existing personal theories. Both in-therapy behavioral practice and extra-therapeutic experience with new ways of behaving ... consolidate the revised theories and the altered actions and action tendencies associated with them. ... Ultimately, clients who have benefited from psychotherapeutic conversations and activities are potentially capable of contributing to the personal, interpersonal, social, and

cultural contexts in which they exist in ways that alter ... their experiences in them.

(Martin, 1994, pp. 101–102)

This was the theory of how psychotherapy works that I extracted from the extensive program of research I conducted with my colleagues at the University of Ontario from the fall of 1983 to the spring of 1991. In my 1994 book, I also was careful to note that the extent of client change and benefit that occurs even in what is deemed to be successful psychotherapy is necessarily dependent on a host of other factors in the lives and life experiences and contexts of clients, factors that might limit and perhaps reverse any gains that were made or might be attributed to their experiences in, and learning from, psychotherapy per se. I subsequently elaborated these and other lessons I extracted from my research experiences at UWO in a chapter published in 1995 contained in a volume I co-edited with Lisa Tsoi Hoshmand, *Research as Praxis: Lessons from Programmatic Research in Therapeutic Psychology.*

Lisa also had worked in London, Ontario, but before my arrival in 1983. I learned a great deal from her during the time of our later collaboration. She was a student of a mutual friend, Don Polkinghorne, a well-known figure in humanistic, theoretical, and counseling psychology whose friendship and support I was fortunate to enjoy during much of the middle and later years of my career in psychology.

One of the things that amazed me most about my time at Western was how quickly success in academic psychology can be attained (of course, this awareness also indicated how ephemeral any such success can be). I had come to London, Ontario as a relatively unknown academic research psychologist. Less than nine years later, I left Western with a solid reputation as an established researcher in counseling psychology and psychotherapy, with 35 solo and co-authored articles in leading journals of counseling psychology, a few awards from international societies in counseling psychology, membership on three editorial boards of widely recognized and respected journals of counseling psychology, including the *Journal of Counseling Psychology*, and an appointment as Research Editor of the *Journal of Counseling and Development*. In December 1989, I spent an enjoyable and rewarding few weeks before Christmas as an Emens Distinguished Visiting Professor at Ball State University in Muncie, Indiana, writing and interacting with scholars in counseling psychology and psychotherapy like David Dixon, then Chair of the Department of Counseling and Educational Psychology at Ball State.

Perhaps ironically, now that I had established bona fide "chops" as a research psychologist, I began to prefer theoretical work of the sort that appeared in fledgling form, albeit mixed with extensive summaries of empirical research, in my 1994 book *The Construction and Understanding of Psychotherapeutic Change.* I also found myself preoccupied with understanding more clearly what I had come to regard as the inevitable limits of empirical, scientific psychology as conventionally practiced. Not only could psychological research (especially in the more social and applied area of psychology) produce no truly general findings (certainly no laws), it displayed a historical and continuing failure to come to grips with what I believed to be its most fundamental subject matter—*people and their lives.* As successful as our research group on counseling psychology and psychotherapy had been at Western, and even after writing a reasonably satisfying account of a theory of psychotherapeutic change that for me was the major outcome of all the empirical work we had completed, I still felt that something central to my interests in psychology was missing. The more I thought about it, the missing and central piece was an understanding of people as persons, whose lives unfolded within particular life situations in interaction with other people.

As the decade of the 1980s drew to an end, I was loosening my ties to those aspects of cognitive psychology I had initially found useful in combating the failures of behaviorism to take human language, agency, and reasoning seriously. Under the influence of Harré (1984) and Taylor (1985) and with a more thorough study of earlier writings by Vygotsky (1986), I was beginning my conversion to the study of persons, a study to which I would devote the rest of my career. Having been introduced to classic works in British philosophy by two friends at UWO, Jim Sanders and John McPeck, I added further to my concerns about cognitive psychology's reduction of persons to their purported mental interiors. I found the writings of Gilbert Ryle (1949) and Peter Strawson (1959) especially informative and convincing.

Another major influence on my thinking about psychology at this time was the historian and philosopher of psychology Sigmund Koch (like me, a one-time dyed-in-the-wool behaviorist) who had come to consider behaviorism and the mistaken idea of a scientific psychology in the manner of physical science to evidence what he called "ameaningful thinking." In his Morrison Lecture to the Scripps Institute in 1961, Koch described psychologists' institutionalized failure to think clearly or at all about people as their core subject matter and the primary object of their psychological inquiries as a vivid example of "ameaningful thinking":

> When we think ameaningfully, there is a tendency to defend ourselves against the object of thought or inquiry, rather than to embrace it; to maintain from it a circumspect distance rather than to become host to it; to master the object of inquiry rather than to understand it; to engage in transaction with it rather than in a love affair; to use it rather than to savor it … to suppose that the object of inquiry is an ungainly and annoying

irrelevance and that knowledge can be gained by fiat. ... Psychology exhibits the trend in an extreme form ... [It is] unique in the extent to which its institutionalization preceded its content and its methods preceded its problems.

(Koch, 1999, *Psychology in Human Context: Essays in Dissidence and Reconstruction*, pp. 234–235)

Koch goes on to say that "Method-fetishism in the degree to which it exists in psychology means, in short, that investigators have little respect for the objects of inquiry, the subject matter of their discipline" (p. 250) and that "psychologists must finally accept the circumstance that extensive and important sectors of psychological study require modes of inquiry more like those of the humanities than the sciences" (p. 416).

With all of this, I was beginning to feel like I finally might be closing in on some of what I was looking for when I first decided to pursue psychology as a means of understanding myself and others like me.

At Western, I had learned a great deal about the nature, limitations, and possibilities of psychotherapy and psychotherapeutic change, but in the final analysis it was people, individually and collectively, who changed. A more complete and genuine understanding of human learning and change required an understanding of people themselves. The promise of such an understanding was what first had drawn me to psychology as an undergraduate before I came under the thrall of the possibility of a science of human behavior, as if behavior could be studied independently of the persons who exhibited it.

During my first stint at SFU, I had been so preoccupied with learning, and needing, to be a successful academic psychologist that any line of thinking that did not lead directly to conducting publishable empirical research was, at least for the most part, pushed firmly out of mind. At Western, with tenure and promotions behind me, I had been able to plan and execute a research program of my own choosing, in close cooperation with outstanding colleagues and friends. Nonetheless, I now realized with considerable dismay that what I was really looking for had still evaded me. What I was after was a chance to immerse myself in the study of human beings as persons with unique capabilities to understand themselves and others, to make decisions and choices, to cooperate and collaborate with others, and to act (individually and collectively) in ways that made a productive difference in their lives and in the lives of others. Koch's admonishments concerning the ameaningful thought and method-fetishes of institutionalized psychology were ringing ever louder in my ears. What could I do to embrace persons and their lives as the core subject matter of psychology and counter the institutionalized tendencies to which Koch referred so disparagingly, but so eloquently and convincingly?

Reading Koch, Harré, Taylor, Ryle, Strawson, Vygotsky, and others like Roy Bhaskar (1989) and John Greenwood (1989, 1991) helped me to clarify what I still found to be inadequate about the implicit conception of persons as understood within the general social-cognitive framework that influenced my and colleagues' work at the University of Western Ontario. The conceptual lenses, implicitly quasi-causal models, and methodological and analytic innovations we employed to analyze therapist and client interactions, ratings, and reactions to psychotherapy were useful tools for understanding some aspects of psychotherapeutic change, but they inevitably reduced the personhood and experiences of those whose interactions and reactions we studied. In our research, the question of exactly how therapy fits into the total life experiences and personhood of those we studied was mostly sidestepped.

It is persons, not variables (like "client and therapist ratings" and "numbers of important events") and constructs (like "conceptual maps" and "personal theories"), who hope, strive, remember, decide, learn, and change. Instead of focusing our attention primarily on persons and the life contexts within which their concerns and difficulties arise, we were focused on putative social-cognitive mechanisms (e.g., "memorability of metaphoric language") and purported processes of change (e.g., "memory-mediated revision of personal theories"). Much of what I wrote in *The Construction and Understanding of Psychotherapeutic Change* retained and reflected the reductive flavor of conventional psychological discourse—discourse that often can mislead and much as inform.

One typically unnoticed way in which psychological discourse can mislead is to encourage confusion about what are genuinely empirical findings and what are logical and conceptual implications of the discursive practices of research psychologists. The Norwegian psychologist Jan Smedslund (1979) was one of the first to argue that many psychological findings are conceptual and logical as much or more than they are empirical. Recently, in April 2019, I referred to my research at the University of Western Ontario when I introduced Jan to an audience at Simon Fraser University who had gathered to hear him speak. After a few remarks about Jan's important contributions to theoretical psychology, I illustrated his main point about the logical, conceptual nature of many empirical results in psychology by describing results from my research on psychotherapy at Western during the 1980s. I said:

> As Jan would be the first to tell you, it does not and should not take years of empirical inquiry to conclude that therapists and clients view psychotherapy as more effective if they work well together and agree about what is significant and important in their interactions.

Even though I think there is more to the conclusions I reached in my 1994 book than tautology and conceptual implication, there can be no denying that

Jan has a point. Think for example of Al Bandura's research on self-efficacy that consistently links human performance to self-efficacy judgments of human performers. The results of such research often are expressed in words such as: "When added to past performance data, self-efficacy ratings predicted performance beyond what was predicted by past performance alone." However, as Jan (Smedslund, 1979) has pointed out, it is not surprising to "discover" that people who think they can do something at a particular level are more likely to do it at that level than people who think they are incapable of doing so. Clearly, there may be exceptions, as when an athlete who is not feeling well and seems not ready to compete performs much better than she ever has performed before. However, these are the exceptions that call out for explanation—explanation that is often found in particular circumstances unique to that unlikely performance. It would be very strange if such anomalies were statistically more likely than performance being consistent with a performer's assessment of and confidence that she can perform at a given level. Otherwise, none of us would know what we are talking about in our typical discourse about persons and their performances. For example, we would be incapable of distinguishing between something anomalous and something expected.

Upon close examination, much of what we think we know is contained in our linguistic and discursive practices—practices in which we participate continuously. Many of the findings psychologists claim are validated by empirical research are, in fact, rendered true prior to any such research by the ways in which terms are defined and used in common parlance. Listening to Jan's recent talk, I found myself wondering again how much of what I had learned about psychotherapeutic change was related directly to the empirical research I had undertaken and how much I had drawn from my everyday experiences of life as a psychologist and person, within and outside of the conventions, practices, and mantras of formal, disciplinary psychology.

Thinking about psychological science and its claims to be grounded in empirical evidence more generally, I also found myself seriously contemplating the unlikely idea enshrined in the scientist-practitioner model of applied psychology that psychological science is capable of supporting professional psychological interventions with persons who somehow are considered to be quite highly determined for the purposes of psychological science yet also are understood, at least implicitly, as active agents when it comes to applying what they take from psychological interventions. At the very least, I thought psychology owed its practitioners and consumers an explanation of the Janus-faced person its scientific and professional arms seemed to require. It appeared more than a bit odd, and a tad self-serving, to view persons as potentially active agents capable of taking charge of their lives if, and only if, they are readily amenable to the science-based administrations of professional psychologists. This problematic tension, which arose from reflecting on my research on counseling and psychotherapy at Western and conversations with others like Albert Ellis, would prove to be yet another link to the work on personhood and agency that awaited my arrival back at SFU.

For back to SFU was where I was headed. Wyn's father and my father died during the late 1980s and our mothers were not well. With our oldest child completing elementary school, we realized that if we ever were to return to Western Canada we would need to do so before life with teenage children would keep us in London, Ontario. After it became known to some of my friends and previous colleagues at SFU that I was considering an offer from an American university, I was asked if I would be interested in returning to SFU. Thus, by the time my book *The Construction and Understanding of Psychotherapeutic Change* was published, Wyn and I, with our three children, had returned to Simon Fraser University.

References

Bhaskar, R. (1989). *Reclaiming reality*. London: Verso.

Greenwood, J. D. (1989). *Explanation and experiment in social psychological science: Realism and the social constitution of action*. New York: Springer-Verlag.

Greenwood, J. D. (1991). *Relations and representations: An introduction to the philosophy of social psychological science*. New York: Routledge.

Harré, R. (1984). *Personal being: A theory for personal psychology*. Cambridge, MA: Harvard University Press.

Haynes, C. R., Marx, R. W., Martin, J., Wallace, L., Merrick, R., & Einarson, T. L. (1983). Rational-emotive counselling and self-instruction training for test anxious high school students. *Canadian Counsellor, 18*, 31–38.

Hoshmand, L. T., & Martin, J. (Eds.). (1995). *Research as praxis: Lessons from programmatic research in therapeutic psychology*. New York: Teachers College Press, Columbia University.

Koch, S. (1999). *Psychology in human context: Essays in dissidence and reconstruction* (D. Finkleman & F. Kessel, Eds.). Chicago, IL: The University of Chicago Press.

Martin, J. (1990). Individual differences in client reactions to counselling and psychotherapy: A challenge for research. *Counseling Psychology Quarterly, 3*(1), 67–83.

Martin, J. (1992). Cognitive-mediational research on counseling and psychotherapy. In S. G. Toukmanian & D. L. Rennie (Eds.), *Psychotherapy process research* (pp. 108–133). Newbury Park, CA: Sage.

Martin, J. (1994). *The construction and understanding of psychotherapeutic change: Conversations, memories, and theories*. New York: Teachers College Press, Columbia University.

Martin, J., Cummings, A. L., & Hallberg, E. T. (1992). Therapists' intentional use of metaphor: Memorability, clinical impact, and possible epistemic/motivational functions. *Journal of Consulting and Clinical Psychology, 60*(1), 143–145.

Martin, J., & Hiebert, B. A. (1985). *Instructional counseling: A method for counselors.* Pittsburgh, PA: The University of Pittsburgh Press.

Martin, J., Martin, W., Meyer, M., & Slemon, A. G. (1986). An empirical investigation of the cognitive mediational paradigm for research on counseling. *Journal of Counseling Psychology, 33*(2), 115–123.

Martin, J., Martin, W., & Slemon, A. G. (1989). Cognitive-mediational models of action-act sequences in counseling. *Journal of Counseling Psychology, 36*(1), 8–16.

Martin, J., Slemon, A. G., Hiebert, B., Hallberg, E. T., & Cummings, A. L. (1989). Conceptualizations of novice and experienced counselors. *Journal of Counseling Psychology, 36*(4), 395–400.

Martin, J., & Stelmaczonek, K. (1988). Participants' identification and recall of important events in counseling. *Journal of Counseling Psychology, 35*(4), 385–390.

Ryle, G. (1949). *The concept of mind.* London: Hutchinson's University Library.

Smedsland, J. (1979). Between the analytic and the arbitrary: A case study of psychological research. *Scandinavian Journal of Psychology, 20*(1), 129–140.

Strawson, P. (1959). *Individuals: An essay in descriptive metaphysics.* London: Routledge.

Taylor, C. (1985). The person. In M. Carrithers, S. Collins & S. Lukes (Eds.), *The category of the person: Anthropology, philosophy, history* (pp. 257–281). Cambridge: Cambridge University Press.

Vygotsky, L. (1986). *Thought and language* (A. Kozulin, Ed.). Cambridge, MA: MIT Press. (Original work published 1934).

5 Finding a Home
In Full Pursuit of Persons

Upon my return to SFU, I worked in the Counselling and Educational Psychology Programs in the Faculty of Education and also taught in the History and Theory of Psychology Program of the Department of Psychology. By splitting my teaching between Education and Psychology, I avoided any work in the professional education of teachers, for which I still felt unprepared. My work with the SFU Theory and History of Psychology group reflected a major change in my professional career and focus.

Throughout the previous nine years at UWO, even while still engaged in the program of research on counseling and psychotherapy described in the previous chapter, I was turning with more and more interest to the theory and history of psychology. It was here I thought I would find keys to the understanding of persons, their development, and their lives that I finally felt ready and able to pursue. Some very initial ideas that heralded this later-career shift in my scholarly interests and work are mentioned in embryonic form in my 1994 psychotherapy book:

> Human experience occurs in the context of cultural, social, interpersonal, and personal conversations, and the practical activities associated with these conversations. Human thought and forms of understanding, both conceptual and practical, are appropriated (internalized) from the conversations and practical activities within which human experience unfolds. Memories of experience in conversations and associated practical activities are primary vehicles for the appropriation of forms of thought and understanding. Personal theories are belief systems based on appropriated forms of thought and understanding. Such theories … support and enable perceptual, experiential, affective, motivational, and cognitive processes (e.g., values, reasons, dispositions, goals, and so forth) on which human actions are based.
>
> (Martin 1994, pp. 100–101)

Readers familiar with the works of Lev Vygotsky, George Herbert Mead, and Rom Harré, will recognize the influence of their writings on this preliminary framing of some of the ideas that would populate my theoretical work upon my return to SFU. These and related influences of a growing number of other sociocultural and discursive theorists of human development and personhood soon would erase any vestiges of cognitive mentalism from my future work.

Settling in upon My Return

During the early and mid-1990s, I settled into life back at SFU and in our new family home overlooking Burrard Inlet in the nearby community of Port Moody, British Columbia. With the aid of grants from the Social Sciences and Humanities Research Council of Canada, I completed qualitative and theoretical analyses of recordings and transcriptions I had brought with me from UWO, and extended my theory of psychotherapeutic change to an analysis of psycho-educational and life learning and change more generally. I also published my psychotherapy book (Martin, 1994), several articles and chapters I had planned prior to coming back to SFU, and a few more based on new work I conducted at SFU. I also settled into my teaching schedule, which included the supervision of several outstanding graduate students, two of whom later became SFU faculty members and colleagues and also worked in the theory and history of psychology—Jeff Sugarman and Kate Slaney. I also published, with Lisa Tsoi Hoshmand, an edited volume, *Research as Praxis: Lessons from Programmatic Research in Therapeutic Psychology* (1995), in which we examined and formulated implications for psychological theory and inquiry more generally of the kind of work I, Lisa, and others had conducted on psychotherapeutic processes and outcomes.

After brief stints in university administration as Director of Undergraduate Programs in the Faculty of Education and Associate Dean of Graduate Studies for the University, in partial repayment to SFU for rehiring me, I shifted my scholarly attention and energies much more fully to my interests in the theory and history of psychology as related to personhood. This did not mean that I ceased to be active on departmental, faculty, and university committees. Throughout the 1990s and into the final years of my second stint at SFU, I was a member of many such committees. I always considered committee duty to fall within a reasonable definition of good citizenship and service to the university community or, perhaps less loftily, I wanted to be seen to do my share of the grunt work. During this time, I served as Chair of the Tenure and Promotion Committee of the Faculty of Education, chaired and oversaw implementation of salary adjustment decisions made by a university-wide Gender Equity Committee, and served as a member of special committees struck by two different SFU Presidents.

One of these committees negotiated with the city of Burnaby and the province of British Columbia to acquire title to lands surrounding SFU on Burnaby Mountain, allowing the university to build housing for students, staff, and faculty, and to develop a residential community with shops and services—proceeds from which would fund various university initiatives. The other President's committee was charged with reconsidering the faculty structure of the university and resulted in the movement of some departments and programs to different faculties and the establishment of two entirely new faculties: a Faculty of Communication, Art and Technology and a Faculty of Environment.

The overall goal of my work in the theory and history of personhood from the mid-1990s onward was to understand more fully what I now took to be the primary subject matter of psychology—i.e., people themselves. I was consumed with understanding exactly what a "person" is and how we humans develop, act, and experience ourselves as we do. The success of my program of research on psychotherapy and some initial efforts at theorizing personhood during the 1990s sufficed for a new appointment in 2000 as one of five freshly-minted Burnaby Mountain Chairs. Holding this endowed Chair came with reduced teaching and administrative responsibilities that gave me more time for study and writing and greater freedom to take advantage of opportunities for furthering my work, both at SFU and elsewhere. The fact that the funding for the Burnaby Mountain Chairs derived from proceeds reaped from selling accommodations and businesses in the new community surrounding SFU, the construction of which was authorized by the President's committee on which I served, was of course noted by many of my colleagues, universities being what they are. I like to think that I received my Burnaby Mountain Chair solely on scholarly merit, but it would be disingenuous to deny that being an active participant in the governance of the university for the previous several years might have played some part in my appointment.

My work as Associate Dean of Graduate Studies and as a member of several university-wide committees brought me into contact with SFU professors from many different disciplines, exposure that cut through what one SFU administrator of my acquaintance referred to as the "silo problem." In his opinion, this difficulty wedded faculty members to narrow disciplinary towers where they "upped the draw-bridges" and appointed one or two of their members, who were seen as nonessential, to liaise with other administrative types to do general things to keep the university running—things that required no particular expertise, were beneath the dignity of true scholars, and could keep non-scholars gainfully employed. Continuing on, he claimed that the siege mentality bred by the silo system effectively prevented necessary and desirable interdisciplinary initiatives and projects and ensured that the university did little to reinvigorate, let alone reinvent, itself. Whatever the merits and demerits of such views, Simon Fraser prided itself, or some of its senior administrators did, on being less "silo-ed" than most universities—in particular, much less so than its older, more venerated, cross-town rival, the University of British Columbia.

One of my duties as Associate Dean of Graduate Studies was to have a direct hand in administering a small number of interdisciplinary programs that had been developed or cast outside of the "silo system." One of these was SFU's Graduate Liberal Studies Program (GLS), then directed by a musicologist named Donna Zaph, later to become the Director of Graduate Liberal Studies at Duke University (she recently retired from Duke after a very successful career there). At SFU, Donna wanted to build a direct bridge to the University's Graduate Office and asked me if I might be interested in teaching occasionally in SFU's GLS program. It was difficult to say no to Donna and saying yes was one of the best decisions of my career.

Until my retirement at the end of 2018, I taught quite regularly in GLS, sometimes co-teaching with, or working alongside, people who became reliable academic colleagues and friends: Steve Duguid (Humanities), June Sturrock (English), Jerry Zaslove (Humanities & English), and several others. The typical GLS course ranged widely across the arts, humanities, sciences, and social sciences. Courses included "Reflections on Reason and Passion," "Self and Society," "Tradition and Modernity," "Science and Human Values," "Religion and Secular Worldviews," "Liberty and Authority," and "Organizing Social Realities: Gender, Class, Race, and Nation." The students were engaged and motivated, carefully reading five to eight books in a 13-week course was expected and accepted, and discussions typically were animated and focused. For me, GLS provided an important avenue for exploring, probing, and examining critically many of the topics, arguments, and positions I entertained in thinking and writing about persons and the kind of psychology we require.

Developing a Psychology of Personhood

In the fall of 2002, I was appointed as a Visiting Fellow at the Institut für Grenzgebiete der Psychologie und Psychohygiene (Institute for Frontier Areas of Psychology and Mental Health) in Freiburg, Germany, where I worked closely with Harald Atmanspacher, a theoretical physicist who directed that Institute and also held a position in the Max Planck Institute in Munich. Harald was very interested in psychology and we enjoyed many wonderful, and sometimes heated, discussions concerning the nature of persons and the concept of "emergence" in physical and social science (Martin, 2003). Harald, a world-class mountaineer, took Wyn and me for several memorable hikes in the Black Forest and across the border into the Alsace region of France. With our children grown, Wyn was able to accompany me on such ventures and pursue interests of her own.

Through Harald I met Hans Primas, a Swiss physical and theoretical chemist at ETH Zürich, with whom I enjoyed several discussions about the nature of determinism and its limits. Hans once told me that science can explain everything except the behavior of scientists, a more formal statement of which he included in a 2002 chapter, entitled "Hidden Determinism, Probability, and Time's Arrow":

> [W]e assume that the physical system under investigation is governed by strictly deterministic or probabilistic laws. On the other hand, we also have to assume that the experimentalist stands out of these natural laws. The traditional assumption of theoretical physics that the basic deterministic laws are universally and globally valid for all matter thus entails a pragmatic contradiction between theory and practice. *A globally deterministic physics is impossible.*
>
> (Primas, p. 102)

At the very end of this same chapter, Hans adds that "[I]t is very much an open question what form a physical theory including the freedom of action will take" (p. 109). I considered Hans' remarks in light of my ongoing efforts to theorize personhood and subsequently spent many hours thinking about whether and how persons (like Hans' experimentalist) might "stand out of natural laws."

In its early phases, my work on personhood was guided by what I took to be important criticisms of mainstream empirical psychology, especially as mounted by theoretically and historically oriented scholars of psychology like Rom Harré, Kurt Danziger, Ian Hacking, and Sigmund Koch and others like Hans-Georg Gadamer and Charles Taylor. I studied their papers and books closely and oftentimes included readings from them in the classes I taught. I was searching actively for philosophical frameworks that were suitable for understanding social psychological phenomena of personhood such as agency and selfhood. I wanted perspectives that accepted the non-reductive reality and importance of these phenomena without reifying them as mysterious inner or fixed, immutable entities. Roy Bhaskar's critical realism (e.g., *Reclaiming Reality*, 1989) and John Greenwood's social realism and constitutionism (e.g., *Explanation and Experiment in Social Psychological Science: Realism and the Social Constitution of Action*, 1989) were especially useful in this regard. On my interpretation, they complimented Rom Harré's and Charles Taylor's ideas about selfhood and personhood, explaining how these and other social psychological phenomena could be both socially constituted, yet real and influential.

Social constitution differs from social influence or causation in that it connotes the complex enculturation and development of persons through their existence, participation, and active interchange with others within sociocultural traditions and ways of life. Although Harré called his approach social constructionism, he also assumed that persons were active agents, determined by and determining of their life contexts. As already mentioned Rom's book *Personal Being* (1984) had an enormous influence on me, one I was able to acknowledge recently in a chapter I contributed (Martin, 2019) to an edited volume in tribute to Rom's illustrious career as a philosopher of science and psychology at Oxford and Georgetown universities. Rom wrote a response to the various chapters in this book, but did not live to see its publication in 2019. I dislike the thought of no longer seeing his small, dynamic figure chuckling and gesturing enthusiastically in the cut and thrust of debates about how psychology might change its theories and methods.

My closest colleagues at SFU were distinguished educational philosopher and classicist Robin Barrow (who has become a lifelong friend) and two former graduate students, Jeff Sugarman (for whom I acted as senior supervisor of his Ph.D. dissertation), and Kate Slaney (on whose Master's and Ph.D. supervisory committees I served). After completing their doctoral programs, Jeff and Kate joined the permanent faculty at SFU. Much of my later-career theoretical work on the nature and capabilities of persons was conducted with Jeff, whose doctoral thesis was an in-depth comparison, elaboration, and extension of the theories of human agency advanced by Rom Harré and Canadian philosopher Charles Taylor. Since completing his doctoral studies, Jeff has become a close friend and is my most frequent collaborator. He and I still meet regularly to discuss mutual interests and projects, often over lunch, following an hour or so on the tennis courts, something we are both anxious to resume once the current pandemic is managed.

Early in our collaboration, Jeff and I were encouraged in our work by receiving the George Miller Award for an Outstanding Recent Article in General Psychology given by the Society for General Psychology (Division 1 of the American Psychological Association). The piece for which the award was given was published in 1999 in the *Journal of Theoretical and Philosophical Psychology* and was entitled "Psychology's Reality Debate: A 'Levels of Reality' Approach." In this article, we provided a general framework for the theory of personhood we went on to develop in a trilogy of books published between 1999 and 2010. In these books, Jeff and I (assisted by Janny Thompson and Sarah Hickinbottom) developed in detail our conceptions of agency, selfhood, and personhood and discussed the implications of the descriptions and arguments we advanced for psychological theory and inquiry. The three books are *The Psychology of Human Possibility and Constraint* (1999, State University of New York Press), *Psychology and the*

Question of Agency (2003, State University of New York Press), and *Persons: Understanding Psychological Selfhood and Agency* (2010, Springer).

Many of the themes Jeff and I wrote about in these books were elaborated further in relation to other approaches to these topics in two additional volumes I co-edited—*The Sociocultural Turn in Psychology: The Contextual Emergence of Mind and Self* with Suzanne Kirschener (2010, Columbia University Press) and *The Psychology of Personhood: Philosophical, Historical, Social-Developmental, and Narrative Perspectives* with Mark Bickhard (2013, Cambridge University Press). Suzanne, until recently a professor of psychology at the College of the Holy Cross in Worchester, Massachusetts, and I have known each other since the early 1990s through our attendance at meetings of the Society for Theoretical and Philosophical Psychology. I first met Mark Bickhard at a conference in Copenhagen, after which (from 2005–2012) I served as an associate editor for the journal *New Ideas in Psychology*, which Mark co-edited with Robert Campbell. During this same time, I occasionally attended conferences Mark organized in Europe and North America. Both Suzanne and Mark are outstanding scholars and it was an easygoing pleasure to work with them on these projects.

Jeff's and my work on the psychology of personhood reflected the influence of Vygotsky's sociocultural, developmental psychology, early twentieth-century American pragmatic, functionalist psychology and philosophy (especially the writings of George Herbert Mead), Continental hermeneutics (especially the work of Hans Georg Gadamer and Charles Taylor), the hybrid social constructionism of Rom Harré, the social constitutionism of John D. Greenwood, and the humanistic existentialism of Ernest Becker, amongst others. A primary rationale and purpose of our work on personhood has been to combat the tendency in much psychological research and practice to reduce persons to their component parts (e.g., their brains), to liken them to nonhuman animals and machines (e.g., computers), and to otherwise deny their agency and simplify their unique capabilities, such as imagination, perspective taking, and coordination with others. As the history of psychology demonstrates so clearly, such reductionism is associated with attempts to make psychology scientific in the manner of physics. However, nothing of ultimate value to a psychology of persons can be achieved by treating persons as mere physical objects. Certainly the bodies of people are subject to physical and chemical laws, but, as Hans Primas saw clearly, the psychological functioning of persons cannot be studied and understood in the same way as can inanimate objects without reflective consciousness, rational and moral agency, and other social, psychological capabilities unique to persons. Making people small and then trying to do big scientific things with them inevitably courts oversimplification and irrelevance. People, their unique capabilities, and the nature of their existence and circumstances cannot be reduced and ignored if psychology is to provide credible knowledge relevant to helping us live more fulfilling and less troubled lives.

Only persons and their worldly activity are the proper focus for a psychology that aims to enhance our ability to lead productive lives with others. But if psychology is to study and understand persons it must know what persons are. My theoretical writings about persons, much of it with Jeff, treats persons as embodied human beings and reasoning, moral agents with self-consciousness, understanding of self and others, social and psychological identity, and unique linguistic and cultural capabilities that allow us to coordinate our actions and purposes with those of others. These defining characteristics and capabilities of persons emerge developmentally within the worldly activity of biological human beings interactively communicating and coordinating their actions with others and objects in the biophysical and sociocultural contexts we inhabit.

Persons are always embodied, embedded, enactive, and emergent. Selfhood is not traceable to a substantive entity lurking within a deeply psychological interior. It is the first-person experience and understanding of a person's particular existence that emerges through one's ongoing interactive engagements with others. Identity is a person's recognition by others and through others by one's self as an individual with a unique and distinctive autobiography and personality. Rational and moral agency is the deliberative, reflective activity of a person in choosing and executing actions in a way that is not fully determined by factors and conditions other than self-understanding, reasoning, and moral consideration. It is the purposeful action of persons. In their evolution and development, persons as agents are constituted and constantly emergent within their biophysical and sociocultural world. Because persons often act for reasons and purposes, their actions are not reducible to biophysical and sociocultural determinants apart from their personal self-determination. Human action often requires formal and telic explanation in addition to efficient and material explanation.

A New Location and Some New Directions

In 2007, my appointment at SFU was converted to a fulltime position as Burnaby Mountain Chair of Theory and History of Psychology in SFU's Department of Psychology. Perhaps paradoxically, around this same time I abandoned traditional psychological empiricism entirely, even in the supervision of graduate student theses. I devoted myself to work in the theory and history of psychology (especially the psychology of personhood), using philosophical, historical, sociocultural, and biographical perspectives and methods to deepen my understanding of human beings as uniquely capable psychological persons. I now firmly believe that such an understanding can only be glimpsed, if noted at all, through the vast majority of psychologists' experiments, questionnaires, and surveys. Once I was located physically in the Department of Psychology, I was extremely fortunate to be able to work more closely with a small number of SFU faculty who included social psychologist Bill Turnbull, developmental psychologists Bryan Sokol and Jeremy Carpendale, developmental and theoretical psychologist Tim Racine, and of course, Kate Slaney.

My last years at SFU prior to my retirement were also marked by a productive study of social developmental psychology and some critical work in educational psychology as related to my interests in selfhood, agency, and personhood. Many individual conversations and discussions during seminars and reading group meetings with Bryan Sokol, Jeremy Carpendale, Bill Turnbull, Jeff, and Kate were invaluable in advancing my understanding of contemporary social developmental theory in psychology. Robin Barrow and Jeff consistently provided follow-up opportunities, often over a weekly pint at our favorite pub, for me to articulate and refine my understandings. As a result, I was able to piece together an extended theory of ontogeny, which built on Jeff and my previous work on the development of personhood, to explain further the development of important capabilities of persons such as perspective taking, self-consciousness and understanding, moral and rational agency, and autobiographical experience and memory. This was an ontogeny that explained how such capabilities could emerge within everyday social interactivity with others during infancy and childhood in ways that avoided excessive nativism on the one hand and an unyielding social determinism on the other.

A second, and closely related, gift from my seminar discussions concerning the social development of persons was to stimulate and enhance further my interest in and understanding of the work of American pragmatist, George Herbert Mead. When I delivered papers reworking Mead's ideas and adding some of my own, especially concerning the ontogenetic emergence of personhood, at international meetings of the Jean Piaget Society and the International Society for Theoretical Psychology, I met social and developmental psychologist Alex Gillespie. Alex also was doing work on Mead and he and I subsequently developed and published several articles about what we call position exchange theory, which became an important part of my more general approach to the ontogeny of persons. During this same time, I met briefly and became aware of the work of Michael Tomasello who, with his collaborators and students, has contributed incredibly insightful writings concerning the ontogenetic development of persons as uniquely culture-capable, collective agents capable of acting together in ways that dramatically "ratchet up" the speed and force of evolutionary change.

Throughout our work at SFU from the mid-1990s to my retirement from SFU at the end of 2018, Jeff, Kate, and I were supported and assisted in our individual and collaborative work by countless interactions and exchanges with members of the Society for Theoretical and Philosophical Psychology. At annual meetings of the STPP, I learned a great deal from listening to and conversing with Suzanne Kirschner and Mark Freeman at the College of the Holy Cross, Jim Lamiell at Georgetown University, Phil Cushman at Antioch University in Seattle, Blaine Fowers at the University of Miami, Frank Richardson at the University of Texas, Ken Gergen at Swarthmore College, Anna Stetsenko at the City University of New York, Brent Slife and Stephen Yancher at Brigham Young University, Thomas Teo at York University, Sunil Bhatia at Connecticut College, Scott Churchill at the University of Dallas, and many more brilliant scholars who share my interests in understanding persons and their lives. Both Jeff and I served terms as President of STPP and I predict that Kate probably will do the same in the near future.

Closer to home, after returning to SFU I benefitted greatly from being included in the annual meetings and projects of a small group of theoretical psychologists, all located in Western Canada. The Western Canadian Theoretical Psychologists included Charles Tolman, Leo Moss, Hank Stam (founding editor of the journal *Theory & Psychology*), Bill Smythe, and several others, sometimes with an invited international guest or two like John Shotter. For some reason, Canada has produced a disproportionate number of theoretically inclined psychologists. I've often wondered about this and why it might be the case, but there can be no doubt whatsoever of my own debt to the support, encouragement, and insights I received from my involvement in the WCTP.

A Critique of Psychology in Education

In my later university career, I also found time to conduct some critical work in educational psychology that focused on the theoretical, methodological, and practical difficulties created by the excessive individualism that crept into North American psychology during the second half of the twentieth century. I owe Frank Richardson, Blaine Fowers, Phil Cushman, and Robert Bishop a great debt for many animated discussions at meetings of the Society for Theoretical and Philosophical Psychology, some conducted over a single malt or two, that furthered my understanding of the nature and perils of individualism as perpetuated in and through psychological inquiry and theory.

Written with former student Ann-Marie McLellan, whose doctoral work I supervised, *The Education of Selves: How Psychology Transformed Students* (2013) examines the role played by scientific and professional psychology in transforming ideals for student conduct, experience, and goals in American and Canadian schools during the second half of the twentieth century. This was a period and context within which psychological conceptions, measures, research, and interventions related to students' "selves" became highly influential and enshrined in school and classroom rhetoric and practices. Educational goals, policies, and curricula were increasingly focused on the personal development of students as individuals with high levels of self-esteem, self-concept, self-efficacy, and self-regulation. Schools and teachers assumed greater responsibility for ensuring that all students developed as psychological selves—as individuals with the kinds of inner psychological resources that would enable them to lead fulfilling lives, replete with high levels of self-regard, self-understanding, self-confidence, and strategically directed self-interest. Increasingly, psychologists working in schools and the teachers they influence claimed to be able, based on scientific research in psychology, to enhance both the self-expression and self-management of students in ways that would allow them to develop the self-confidence and ability to become enterprising lifelong learners in pursuit of their own interests and concerns.

The problem with all of this was that insufficient attention was being devoted to the cultivation of students' social development, concern for, and abilities to care about and work together with others. For the most part, this was an unintended consequence of the new psychology-fueled importance that educators at all levels of K–12 schooling now attached to students' self-development. An ideal of students as future entrepreneurs driven by self-interest gradually began to replace a more traditional emphasis on students as knowledgeable citizens concerned about, and committed to participation in, their schools and communities. Ann-Marie and I termed this new ideal the "triple-E" student—"expressive, enterprising, and entitled." Perspective taking, social interactivity, and cooperation, which Jeff and I viewed as necessary developmental cornerstones of personhood, were neglected in ways that produced strategically maneuvering students, instrumentally attuned to their own interests and progress. Multifaceted self-understanding and the exercise of essential capabilities of personhood such as moral and rational agency that required active participation, orientation to, and negotiation and cooperation with others were being compromised to make way for a less pluralistic, overriding focus on individual self-promotion and success.

More detailed concerns Ann-Marie and I expressed about psychology's involvement in schools focused on the ways in which psychology promoted a solipsistic individualism by encouraging a focus on students' inner selves and internal structures and processes (such as personal theories, personality structures, and cognitive information processing), presented a narrowly reductive and simplified vision of human life as a mostly individual struggle (often against other's and community values and conventions), and manipulated students in subtle ways to adopt corporate, neoliberal values and means of production and consumption. The overall result was an increasing number of K–12 students with high self-regard, little self-control, and a tendency to narcissistic self-satisfaction and entitlement, who regarded their own emotional reactions as pointing to what was true and whose empathy for others was underdeveloped. Some of these themes subsequently have been developed much more extensively and more broadly applied to society at large by Jeff in his work on psychology and neoliberalism (e.g., Sugarman, 2015).

A Biographical Turn: Position Exchange and Life Positioning Analysis

My second and longest stint at SFU extended from 1991–2018 and was marked by seemingly endless reading, discussion, writing, conferencing, and the publishing of numerous articles, chapters, edited volumes, monographs, and books. The net result was that by 2010, I felt that I had made, with the tremendously important help of close colleagues and collaborators at SFU and beyond, considerable strides in my effort to better understand persons, their capabilities, and their development. Around this time, I decided that I also wanted to do more to apply my and my colleagues' theories of personhood and agency to the intensive study of the lives and experiences of particular individuals. Traditional empirical work in psychology that makes use of statistical aggregation and testing is useless for this purpose (if you don't believe me, perhaps you might believe Marty Byrde, one of the protagonists in the Netflix series *Ozark*, who repeatedly makes reference [e.g., episode 1 of season 3] to the fact that it is possible to use "the law of large numbers" in ways that can yield useful predictions, but impossible to know what any individual might or might not do on any particular occasion). Consequently, I now turned to biography, in particular to a form of psychobiography I developed (making use of Alex's and my theory of position exchange) called Life Positioning Analysis (LPA) (Martin, 2013).

LPA allowed me to incorporate a life-long interest in history and biography into the study of the lives of prominent psychologists and others within the context of the conceptual, theoretical, and developmental work on personhood that had consumed me since returning to SFU in the early 1990s. Since I learned to read, I have been an avid consumer of biographies and autobiographies. As a young child, I read about the lives of famous athletes and related their stories to my own life experiences. Did all-around athlete Jim Thorpe's dad drink as much as mine did? Would I ever have the discipline of decathlete Bob Mathias or the will to overcome injury and tragedy that marked the lives of miler Glenn Cunningham or golfer Ben Hogan? I even asked neighbors to cut their hedges, which surprisingly they did, at a height that would allow me to mimic all-round athlete and track star Babe Didrikson Zaharias' training regimen for running the hurdles.

Since I first fell for psychology, I have read many autobiographical and biographical writings by psychologists. During the 1970s, after I had finished the first two volumes of B. F. Skinner's autobiography, I wrote to him saying how much I had enjoyed them. Perhaps because the external examiner of my doctoral dissertation had been Kenneth MacCorquodale, a student and later friend of Skinner and an influential psychologist in his own right, Skinner was kind enough to respond. In his return letter dated December 13, 1979, he wrote:

> Naturally I am pleased to know that you have enjoyed the first two volumes of my autobiography. I am working on the third, which will be a very difficult volume to write. It will be less personal and more professional, but by that time my life had become primarily professional. It will cover the years 1948 through 1964.

I recall thinking at the time I received and read this letter that I could not imagine and would not want my own life ever to become "less personal and more professional." But, of course, life changes us over the years and for many of us, the mid-40s to mid-50s (Skinner was born in 1904) encompass the busiest period of our professional lives. Some 20 years later, I had a much better sense of what Skinner was trying to tell me.

Whatever their favorite methods for studying the actions and responses of participants in their scientific studies, psychologists obviously prefer biography and autobiography as methods for recording their own and each other's lives. Influential psychologists like Granville Stanley Hall and B. F. Skinner produced multi-volume autobiographies, in which they employ ideas and methods drawn from their psychological theories to interpret their own lives. Since the first volume of *A History of Psychology in Autobiography* appeared in 1930, eight additional volumes in this continuing series have been published, together with numerous sub-disciplinary clones containing the autobiographical memoirs and musings of clinical, developmental, social, narrative, feminist, and other psychologists. Beginning with Freud's psychodynamically interpreted biographical essays on the lives of Leonardo di Vinci and Moses and Carl Jung's biographies of Martin Luther and Mahatma Gandhi, psychologists also have published many biographical and psychobiographical essays on the lives of others, including artists, writers, scientists, politicians, entertainers, celebrities, and athletes. Wonderful contemporary examples of such work include Dan McAdam's *George W. Bush and the Redemptive Dream*, in which McAdams (2011) uses his own "Actor-Agent-Author" developmental theory of personhood to illuminate and explain Bush's decision to invade Iraq, and Joseph Ponterotto's (2012) *A Psychobiography of Bobby Fischer: Understanding the Genius, Mystery, and Psychological Decline of a World Chess Champion*.

Psychologist and biographer Alan Elms (1994) has commented that psychobiography "tests the statistically significant against the personally significant" and declares that he has never encountered "a psychologist ... who could put together a live person from ... statistical body parts and honestly cry out, 'It's alive!'" (p. 13). With the publication in 2005 of the *Oxford Handbook on Psychobiography*, edited by psychologist and biographer Todd Schultz, the close link between the psychology of persons and biography as a time-honored method of advancing our understanding of persons and their lives was further confirmed and advanced.

My own interest in psychologists and their lives has been encouraged over the years by several personal encounters and exchanges with prominent scholars and psychologists like social cognitive researcher and theorist Albert Bandura, rational-emotive psychotherapist Albert Ellis, behaviorist B. F. Skinner, philosopher and psychologist Rom Harré, historian and psychologist Kurt Danziger, and many influential contemporaries of my own generation. When teaching the history of psychology at SFU for many years before my retirement, I often sprinkled my lectures and discussions with anecdotes drawn from such experiences. Of course, by this time I had lived through much of the period that comprised the history of modern psychology. What was history for my students merged with what was personal for me. Many students seemed to resonate with my attempts to enliven the history of psychology with personal, biographical information related to the lives of prominent contributors to that history and to place both the history of psychology and the lives of contributors within the broader sociocultural and political contexts of the relevant historical periods. In 2014, I received SFU's Faculty of Arts and Social Sciences Cormack Teaching Award and the Faculty of Arts and Social Sciences Dean's Medal for Academic Excellence, which I took as further confirmation and support of my overall approach to the history and theory of psychology (both pedagogical and scholarly), especially my contributions to the development of a historical and socioculturally grounded psychology of personhood.

Earlier in 2012, I was elected to membership in the Society for Personology, a group of no more than 30 psychologists interested in the study of persons' lives. At the annual meetings of this group, I was able to benefit greatly from face-to-face discussions about personhood and biography with prominent psychobiographers and narrative psychologists like Alan Elms, Dan McAdams, Amy Demorest, Mac Runyan, Jim Anderson, Nicole Barenbaum, Todd Schultz, Sunil Bhatia, and Mark Freeman. My many discussions with Mark Freeman and reading of his books and several articles have been particularly important in advancing my understanding and use of narratives and forms of life writing such as biography, memoir, and literature as invaluable and indispensable sources of psychological insight about persons and their lives.

My interactions with and learning from Mark and other personologists, coupled with intensive study and archival research on the life of existential humanist Ernest Becker, led to the publication of my first full-length psychobiographical essay in 2014. Becker was a professor in the Department of Political Science, Anthropology, and Sociology at SFU at the time of his death in 1974, a year prior to my initial arrival there in 1975. As a post-doctoral fellow at the University of Alberta I had read Becker's (1973) *Denial of Death*, for which he was awarded the Pulitzer Prize for General Nonfiction in 1974. When I arrived at SFU, I was very disappointed to find no memorials or evidence of his time there and made a promise to remedy this situation at some future time, a time that had now come.

After I published my lengthy biographical essay on Becker and his work in the *Journal of Humanistic Psychology* in January 2014, I received a number of invitations to speak about Becker and his ideas to a variety of groups. The Ernest Becker Foundation (EBF), then headquartered in Seattle under the leadership of Neil Elgee was especially welcoming. I gave a couple of talks in Seattle and also recorded a set of vignettes about Becker and his work that I believe is still available on the EBF website. Neil and other members of the EBF, like Dan Leichty, were extremely helpful and excellent sources of information while I was researching Becker's life. Becker's widow Marie Becker-Pos maintained a close connection with the Seattle group, arranging for the preservation of Becker's working library in a temperature- and humidity-controlled room, with independent access, located in a holiday home, overlooking Lake Samish in Washington State, owned by an EBF supporter.

Buoyed by the success of my study of Becker and drawing on my work on position exchange theory with Alex Gillespie and my development of the method of Life Positioning Analysis, I next conducted a dual psychobiographical study of Ernest Becker and Stanley Milgram (Martin, 2016), focusing on their very different but, in my opinion, nonetheless compatible theories of evil. In a second dual psychobiographical study I examined the lives of B. F. Skinner and Carl Rogers (Martin, 2017), with particular emphasis on their oppositional perspectives concerning personal and societal improvement. I also completed LPAs of the lives of athletes Jim Thorpe (Martin, 2013) and Steve Nash (2016) and still am deciding whether or not to do a third dual LPA study that compares and contrasts their very different lives and paths to athletic triumph, with startlingly different consequences. In May 2015, I was an invited guest professor at the Niels Bohr Center for Cultural Psychology at the University of Aalborg, where I had the opportunity of critically examining and further refining my approach to the study of lives, with the generous assistance of Center Director Jaan Valsiner, Svend Brinkmann, Brady Wagoner, and others.

Position exchange theory (PET) (e.g., Gillespie, 2012; Gillespie & Martin, 2014; Martin & Gillespie, 2010; Martin, 2012) explains how our lifelong immersion within and movement between a wide variety of sociocultural positions contributes to our development as persons with unique capabilities of self and other understanding, perspective taking, agency, imagination, and creativity. As biological human beings, we are born with predispositions to orient to the world, especially to other persons, and to remember some of what we experience. These dispositions are present only in the most rudimentary forms at birth and continue to develop throughout our lives in interaction with the world and others in it (Martin & Gillespie, 2010). In early infancy, children experience pre-reflectively. With frequent and increasing interaction in routine position exchanges with others, they learn to coordinate their participation in simple practices that are repeated over and over again—for example, giving and receiving objects, touching and being touched, observing and performing simple actions, and playing games such as peek-a-boo and hide-and-seek. These experiences of position exchange enable the young child to recall and anticipate being in one position (e.g., seeker) while occupying the other position (e.g., hider). Each social position sustains a distinctive perspective or orientation to act in a particular way. It is movement between social positions that enables the child to integrate perspectives—e.g., anticipating where the hider might be when in the role of seeker, and imagining the other with similar and related anticipations when in the role of hider.

A perspective, understood as an orientation and inclination to act, is an experience. One cannot literally take or have someone else's experience. However, repetitive position exchanges, like that between "hider" and "seeker", enable children to have experiences that are more or less similar. By imaginatively recalling and anticipating social interactions that they have engaged and experienced, children are able to coordinate in more complex ways with others, to sense and understand others' perspectives as similar to and different from their own, and eventually to require less direct interactional experience to understand more of what is going on around them (Gillespie, 2012; Martin & Gillespie, 2010, 2013; Martin, 2012).

When taking the perspective of the other, the child never leaves the domain of her own experience but is able to integrate functionally similar experiences by imaginatively drawing from her personal history of occupying the positions and perspectives she has experienced, which are functionally similar to those of others with whom she has interacted. Understanding integration of perspectives in this way provides a theoretical framework for the emergence of intersubjectivity and the agency it affords. Although actors cannot take each other's perspectives directly, they can quite literally take each other's social positions and thus experience similar perspectives.

With the acquisition of language and the ability to imagine possibilities verbalized, even if not extant in more directly observable ways, the child experiences the social world intersubjectively and interactively (Tomasello, 2019). With age, language, and greater social experience, direct and vicarious, the perspectives and possibilities children can coordinate, imagine, and employ purposefully to guide their actions increase dramatically and become increasingly abstracted. Children become able to reflect, even to critique, their own points of view and opinions, to theorize about others and their life experiences, and to engage in social comparison and assessment. They are able to imagine how things might be different from what they are and react to these and other imaginings as well as to what actually is present and occurring around them. Eventually, their personal history of social interactivity and the intersubjectivity it bequeaths enable increasingly sophisticated capabilities of imagination and interpretation that allow older children, adolescents, and adults to develop longer-term purposes for themselves and make plans to achieve them. As goal-oriented, imaginative, and reflective agents, they are able to develop their own identities and styles, even as they continue to harvest the social and psychological riches available through their coordinated interactivity and intersubjectivity with others. Through these social interactions and experiences, we emerge through childhood and adolescence as persons with distinctive identities, self-awareness, creative possibility, and rational and moral agency. As agents, we are able to exercise some degree of self-determination, even if we do not always think or choose to do so and even as we continue to be shaped and influenced by the words and actions of others and the world around us.

LPA studies individual lives by examining their interactions and relationships with "particular others" embedded within what Mead (1934) called "generalized others." Particular others are influential people in the life of a person. Generalized others are salient aspects of the broader social and cultural contexts within which interactions between the person and others occur. LPA consists of an interpretive, recursive examination of importantly influential relationships between particular and general others throughout the life of a person. First, the person's life narrative is chronologically plotted and searched for patterns of interactivity and position exchange with particular others, especially those that seem be repeated across different phases of the person's life. The meaning and significance of these patterns of interactivity then are interpreted through a parsing of the sociocultural conventions, contexts, and traditions within which they occurred. Finally the interactive, interpersonal patterns and themes that emerge are considered in relation to the existential dimensions that run through the person's life as a whole. Such consideration links patterns and contexts of position exchange and life positioning to the works and projects to which the agentive capabilities and creative urges of the individual have been devoted. These are the activities and creations that have given meaning and significance to the life of the person and stand as the person's legacy.

Although I initially developed LPA to study individual lives (Martin, 2013), I also have used it to compare and contrast the life positioning and creative projects of pairs of individuals who share related life contexts and interests. In my studies of Becker and Milgram (Martin, 2016) and of Rogers and Skinner (Martin, 2017), I linked prototypic and often repeated interpersonal interactions and social position exchanges experienced by each of these individuals to the theoretical frameworks and methodological practices they employed in their psychological inquiries and theories.

For example, Rogers' early life interactions within his family displayed a social imbalance that positioned him primarily in the role of listener as opposed to the role of speaker. This imbalance was apparent in his interactions with his parents and older siblings and was sustained by the family's religious convictions that included the ideal "generalized other" of the good, obedient child leading a life of piety that manifests in submission to others and a higher power. This imbalance resulted in a preferred social demeanor in which young Carl kept his feelings to himself and tended to his own upsets and joys while carefully observing and actively listening to others. This characteristic positioning and social posture are readily evident in Rogers' nondirective approach to psychotherapy. However, later in life when he moved to California and became involved in the encounter group movement, he eventually was able to move more easily between positions of active listening to others and genuine expression of his own feelings and experiences. This personal change was intertwined with his mature work in developing person-centered therapy.

In contrast, the position exchange most central to Skinner's personal development and later career was a shift from being controlled by others and his social context to gaining control over his social life by arranging conditions supportive of such a shift. These often involved designing and building devices to aid the desired change. In one such instance, he avoided his mother's disapproval for failing to hang up his pajamas by installing a system of pulleys and written reminders, which was mechanically operated by the opening and closing of his bedroom door. Later in his life and professional career, Skinner was to design several devices and systems, from his laboratory "operant conditioning chambers" to his literary blueprint for a utopian community, to support his experiments and projects. In such examples, it is possible to glimpse the important roles played by incomplete and reciprocal patterns of position exchange in the lives and creative accomplishments of two of America's most famous psychologists, whose life work also reflected major themes of freedom and control in American life more generally.

Whatever biological determinants might have played a role in the lives and accomplishments of Rogers and Skinner, there can be little doubt about the developmental importance of the particular interpersonal, social, and broader cultural contexts within which Skinner and Rogers developed both personally and professionally. Their lives demonstrate not only the ways in which the happenings and contexts of our lives give rise to our interests and projects, but how these interests and projects feed back into those life contexts and enable further developments, in this case important developments in twentieth-century psychology that continue to reverberate in our present ways of thinking about our actions and experiences and about our individual and collective futures.

LPA and other biographical studies require both inference and interpretation. However, this does not mean that these studies are unduly subjective in the sense that any and all interpretations will do or are equivalent. Many lives, including those of Rogers and Skinner, leave wide trails of documentary evidence concerning the events, accomplishments, relationships, interests, concerns, and projects that characterize them, and any viable biographical inquiry is necessarily constrained by such evidence.

An unexpected pleasure of my biographical research and writing, both before and after developing LPA, was the conduct of archival research. Whether working through the collection of Ernest Becker's papers and materials in the Rare Book and Manuscript Collection on the sixth floor of Columbia University's Butler Library or combing through boxes of the Milgram Papers in the archival research room on the ground floor of Yale University's Sterling Memorial Library, I have found the experience of archival research to be inordinately satisfying—a kind of detective work without attendant danger. After securing your valuables and other paraphernalia in a locker, you continue with your laptop (and camera or cellphone as non-flash photographs are permitted) to a vacant spot in the reading room where you wait impatiently for the materials you have ordered to be delivered to your table or work station. Although you previously have combed through the online finding aids and ordered the boxes you want to examine, you never know exactly what you will find in them and the files they contain. With sharpened pencils, writing pads, and forms supplied by the archive, you work through the files and boxes, making notes and recording information, and carefully inserting tags and markers that will allow archival staff to duplicate any materials of which you would like to retain copies. While doing so, you experience the archive—typically the appearance of the well-oiled wood, the feel of the weathered leather of your chair, and the slightly musty, unmistakable smell of old papers and books. I often feel like a child embarking on a great adventure. Until I arise from several hours thus immersed, with aching back and blurry eyes.

When working on Becker, I became transfixed with knowing exactly what his religious views were, to the point that I could hardly sleep, would skip breakfast, and be lined up "ready to take up the chase" as Butler Library opened for the day. Once, in the reading room of the Bibliothèque de Genève, while researching a chapter on Jean-Jacques Rousseau, which I co-wrote with my oldest son for a book on the philosophy of education (Martin & Martin, 2010), I came across a note a previous researcher had left inserted in the original hand-written copy (known as the Favre Manuscript) of Rousseau's *Émile*, which somehow had evaded detection and removal by the archivists. The note, written in French, alerted fellow researchers to the existence of some unprocessed materials about Rousseau that were piled up, awaiting sorting, in one of the library's attics. After treating one of the archivists to an end-of-work-day drink at a nearby wine bar, I was able to examine these off-the-record materials and found an anonymous draft of a manuscript detailing how Rousseau's ideas about education had flowed to John Dewey through the intermediaries of historically well-known educators like Pestalozzi and Froebel and their students. This was a story I knew in broad outline, but the finding of this manuscript, supplemented by further confirmatory exploration at the Geneva Library and elsewhere, gave the chapter we eventually produced more intellectual heft than it otherwise might have had. Over the years, I've grown to love archival spaces and the anticipation of discovery that attends archival research. In my retirement I occasionally make a point of looking through local municipal and regional archives just to see what might turn up.

One satisfying and unexpected result of my work with Alex Gillespie on position exchange theory and its incorporation into my work on life positioning analysis has been the positive reception of this line of inquiry by theorists and students of human creativity like Michael Hanson and Vlad Glăveanu. Vlad has been especially supportive and encouraging, inviting me to contribute chapters and entries on Life Positioning Analysis and position exchange theory to two handbooks he has edited on creativity for Palgrave-Macmillan (Martin, 2016, 2019). Jeff and I included a section on creativity and innovation in the first of our trilogy of books on various aspects of personhood and my reading of biographies and autobiographies inevitably kept me interested in these topics. However, to be encouraged and given the opportunity to revisit these matters through the lenses of PET and LPA was an unexpected and hugely enjoyable experience. I now keep abreast of developments in creativity research and theory as an associate member of Vlad's Center for Creativity and Innovation at Webster University Geneva.

Rounding out a Career

In many ways, the academic year of 2015–2016 capped my career as a university scholar. This was the year in which Jeff, Kate, and I co-edited the first handbook ever to be published on theoretical and philosophical psychology

(*The Wiley Handbook of Theoretical and Philosophical Psychology*), a volume in which all contributors, including us, described philosophical, historical, narrative, sociocultural, and other approaches to theoretical psychology and theoretically informed inquiry in psychology. Later in the summer of 2016, I was honored with the Award for Distinguished Lifetime Contributions to Philosophical and Theoretical Psychology by the Society for Theoretical and Philosophical Psychology. Fittingly, the brief ceremony at which I received this award was held in August in Toronto and the person who presented me with the award was my good friend and colleague, then President of the Society for Theoretical and Philosophical Psychology, Mark Freeman.

During my three-year phased retirement from SFU in 2016–2018, I turned my attention to "life writing" and "the psychological humanities" more generally. My most recent academic article appeared in 2020 in the *Review of General Psychology*, and called for a psychology of persons and their lives that would make extensive use of different modes of life writing including biography and psychobiography. These themes also are discussed in my latest scholarly book, an edited volume with Jeff Sugarman—*A Humanities Approach to the Psychology of Personhood* (Sugarman & Martin, 2020). Since completing our trilogy of books on selfhood, agency, and personhood, Jeff and I continue to collaborate occasionally and continue to enjoy many lively conversations about our current lives and projects. In recent years, it has given me great pleasure to witness Jeff's important and exceptional work as an independent scholar. I find particular insight and merit in his further development and extension of Canadian philosopher Ian Hacking's ideas and methods of historical ontology and in his thorough and penetrating analyses of contemporary neoliberalism and how deeply psychology is implicated in its theories and practices.

In addition to my own later life writings, for the last five years of my university career I served as the founding editor for the *Palgrave Studies in the Theory and History of Psychology*, a position I vacated when I retired and handed off to Thomas Teo of York University. During my tenure as editor, I published 13 books that I like to think might not have been published had I not encouraged, supported, and editorially assisted their completion and production. Some of these books were written by friends and colleagues like Thomas himself, Kate Slaney, Jim Lamiell, Tom Strong, and Blaine Fowers. Others were written by a group of younger scholars whose work I find innovative and important, taking the history and theory of psychology to places, and by means, that I had not imagined possible. These include Wahbie Long, Michael Hanson, Kieran McNally, Gavin Sullivan, Vanessa Lux and Sigrid Weigel, and Heather Macdonald, David Goodman, and Brian Becker. I can think of no other facilitative position or function (with the exception of working with the occasional exceptionally talented graduate student) I enjoyed more than having had the privilege of ushering these books into existence and dissemination.

Yet, my primary focus since my retirement has been to continue to promote a genuinely non-reductive, non-scientistic psychology of persons and their lives. My recent publication in the *Review of General Psychology* (Martin 2020) is a proposal to make persons and their lives the primary focus of psychological theory and inquiry. In this article, I note that the concept of a person does not equate with the concept of a human being understood as a biophysical, substantive entity. "Person" is not a substance concept. Nonetheless, one's identity as a "person" requires one's identity as an individual human being with a distinctive range of capabilities. These include an ability to act based on reason, a personal sense of identity that requires a substantial autobiographical awareness, self-consciousness and the ability to self-ascribe through reason and will, and the ability to incorporate into an individual personality descriptions and practices drawn from the social context of an individual's life experience with others. Human beings are social animals born into a web of familial, communal, social, cultural, and moral concerns and relations.

It is the embeddedness of human beings and their actions within complex norms, conventions, routines, and interactions with others that enables the identification of persons as rational and moral beings. It is through interacting within such contexts that persons are constituted and can be identified by others because of appearance, voice, manner, and style. Unfolding within human culture, the development of children's abilities to cooperate with each other takes a unique ontogenetic form. By the age of six, children are able to operate not only as individual agents but also as collective agents with shared understanding and socio-moral values. It is this coordinative feature of human individual and collective existence that enables cultural practices of teaching and learning unique to human sociocultural transmission and development. These coordinating practices accelerate the development of human beings as persons. They permit new forms "of cooperation with almost total interdependence among individuals" (Tomasello, 2019, p. 342) and the emergence of a shared intentionality that allows us to act jointly within partnerships, groups, and larger sociocultural units to fashion and extend evolving forms of sociality.

Empirical evidence of the unique sociocultural capabilities of persons to coordinate their purposes, plans, and projects are all around us (e.g., urban planning, rule-based community life, communication technologies and infrastructures, libraries, museums, airports—the list goes on and on). It is an overwhelming empirical fact that members of no other species, primate or not, have taken even the first steps toward such complex and powerfully influential sociocultural phenomena—phenomena that are both convention-based, like languages, and that meld material structures with protocols for their use, like convention centers and planetariums.

A psychology of persons recognizes that human beings have evolved and developed ontogenetically as beings with distinctive capabilities of individual and collective, rational and moral agency. Psychology should embrace, not reduce, the complexities of personhood. It should be fueled by purposes of understanding what we are and how we might contribute to human flourishing across our similarities and differences. Psychology should focus on persons without minimizing our distinctive capabilities and accomplishments. Such a psychology ought to draw on scientific, artistic, and humanistic considerations that take full cognizance of our historical, sociocultural, political, economic, and moral contexts by employing a multi-perspectival array of theories, methods, and critical considerations. Only then will psychology finally get its core subject matter, *persons and their lives*, right.

If I succeed in some small way in contributing to a genuinely non-reductive and non-scientistic psychology of persons and their lives that employs methods of life study appropriate to its subject matter, I will be well satisfied. This is where I have arrived and it feels like the right thing for me to do. In fact, it's where I've wanted to be for a long time. But, I don't begrudge the time it has taken me to get here. The longer the struggle, the sweeter the ride, or so I tell myself.

References

Becker, E. (1973). *The denial of death*. New York: Free Press.

Bhaskar, R. (1989). *Reclaiming reality*. London: Verso.

Elms, A. C. (1994). *Uncovering lives: The uneasy alliance of biography and psychology*. New York: Oxford University Press.

Gillespie, A. (2012). Position exchange: The social development of agency. *New Ideas in Psychology*, *30*(1), 32–46.

Gillespie, A., & Martin, J. (2014). Position exchange theory: A socio-material basis for discursive and psychological positioning. *New Ideas in Psychology*, *32*, 73–79.

Greenwood, J. D. (1989). *Explanation and experiment in social psychological science: Realism and the social constitution of action*. New York: Springer-Verlag.

Harré, R. (1984). *Personal being: A theory for individual for individual psychology*. Harvard: Harvard University Press.

Hoshmand, L. T., & Martin, J. (Eds.). (1995). *Research as praxis: Lessons from programmatic research in therapeutic psychology*. New York: Teachers College Press, Columbia University.

Kirschner, S., & Martin, J. (Eds.). (2010). *The sociocultural turn in psychology: The contextual emergence of mind and self*. New York: Columbia University Press.

Martin, J. (1994). *The construction and understanding of psychotherapeutic change: Conversations, memories, and theories.* New York: Teachers College Press, Columbia University.

Martin, J. (2003). Emergent persons. *New Ideas in Psychology, 21*(2), 85–99.

Martin, J. (2012). Coordinating with others: Outlining a pragmatic, perspectival psychology of personhood. *New Ideas in Psychology, 30*(1), 131–143.

Martin, J. (2013). Life positioning analysis: An analytic framework for the study of lives and life narratives. *Journal of Theoretical and Philosophical Psychology, 33*(1), 1–17.

Martin, J. (2014). Ernest Becker at SFU (1969–1974). *Journal of Humanistic Psychology, 54*(1), 66–112.

Martin, J. (2016). Ernest Becker and Stanley Milgram: Twentieth century students of evil. *History of Psychology, 19*(1), 3–21.

Martin, J. (2016). Position exchange, life positioning, and creativity. In V. Glăveanu (Ed.), *The Palgrave handbook of creativity and culture research* (pp. 243–262). London: Palgrave Macmillam.

Martin, J. (2017). Carl Rogers' and B. F. Skinner's approaches to personal and societal improvement: A study in the psychological humanities. *Journal of Theoretical and Philosophical Psychology, 37*(4), 214–229.

Martin, J. (2019). Life positioning analysis: Sociality, materiality, ad creativity in the lives of Carl Rogers and B. F. Skinner. In I. Labuda & V. Glăveanu (Eds.), *The Palgrave handbook of social creativity research* (pp. 109–124). Cham, Switzerland: Palgrave Macmillan.

Martin, J. (2019). Rom Harré on personal agency. In B. A. Christensen (Ed.), *The second cognitive revolution: A tribute to Rom Harré* (pp. 35–42). Cham, Switzerland: Springer.

Martin, J. (2020). A proposal for a general psychology of persons and their lives. *Review of General Psychology, 24*(2), 110–117.

Martin, J., & Bickhard, M. H. (Eds.). (2013). *The psychology of personhood: Philosophical, historical, social-developmental, and narrative perspectives.* Cambridge, England: Cambridge University Press.

Martin, J., & Cox, D. (2016). Positioning Steve Nash: A theory-driven, social psychological and biographical study of creativity in sport. *The Sport Psychologist, 30*(4), 388–398.

Martin, J., & Gillespie, A. (2010). A neo-Meadian approach to human agency: Relating the social and the psychological in the ontogenesis of perspective coordinating persons. *Integrative Psychological and Behavioral Science, 44*(3), 252–272.

Martin, J., & Gillespie, A. (2013). Position exchange theory and personhood. In J. Martin & M. H. Bickhard (Eds.), *The psychology of personhood: Philosophical, historical, social-developmental, and narrative perspectives* (pp. 147–164). Cambridge, England: Cambridge University Press.

Martin, J., & Martin, N. (2010). Rousseau's Émile and educational legacy. In R. Bailey, D. Carr & R. Barrow (Eds.), *The Sage Handbook of philosophy of education* (pp. 85–98). London: Sage.

Martin, J., & McLellan, A. (2013). *The education of selves: How psychology transformed students.* New York: Oxford University Press.

Martin, J., & Sugarman, J. (1999). Psychology's reality debate: A "levels of reality" approach. *Journal of Theoretical and Philosophical Psychology, 19*(2), 177–194.

Martin, J., & Sugarman, J. (1999). *The psychology of human possibility and constraint.* Albany, NY: State University of New York Press.

Martin, J., Sugarman, J., & Hickinbottom, S. (2010). *Persons: Understanding psychological selfhood and agency.* New York: Springer.

Martin, J., Sugarman, J., & Slaney, K. L. (Eds.) (2015). *Wiley handbook of theoretical and philosophical psychology: Methods, approaches and new directions for social science.* Chichester, England: Wiley Blackwell.

Martin, J., Sugarman, J., & Thompson, J. (2003). *Psychology and the question of agency.* Albany, NY: State University of New York Press.

McAdams, D. P. (2011). *George W. Bush and the redemptive dream: A psychological portrait.* New York: Oxford University Press.

Mead, G. H. (1934). *Mind, self, and society: From the standpoint of a social behaviorist.* (C. Morris, Ed.). Chicago, IL: University of Chicago Press.

Ponterotto, J. G. (2012). *A psychobiography of Bobby Fischer: Understanding the genius, mystery, and psychological decline of a world chess champion.* Springfield, IL: Thomas.

Primas, H. (2002). Hidden determinism, probability, and time's arrow. In H. Atmanspacher & R. Bishop (Eds.), *Between chance and choice: Interdisciplinary perspectives on determinism* (pp. 89–114). Exeter, UK: Imprint Academic.

Schultz, W. T. (2005). *Handbook of psychobiography.* New York: Oxford University Press.

Sugarman, J. (2015). Neoliberalism and psychological ethics. *Journal of Theoretical and Philosophical Psychology, 35*(2), 103–116.

Sugarman, J., & Martin, J. (2020). *A humanities approach to the psychology of personhood.* London: Routledge.

Tomasello, M. (2019). *Becoming human: A theory of ontogeny.* Cambridge, MA: Harvard University Press.

6 Retrospective

Reaching for a Psychology of Persons

At this writing, I am 69 years of age, and a year and a half into a full retirement from the day-to-day demands of a paid university position. Free from teaching, graduate student supervision, meetings, and the surprisingly numerous and onerous bits and pieces of administrative activity that attend contemporary academic life, I can do pretty much whatever I want, subject to the vagaries of health, mood, and life with family and friends. I spent the first year of my retirement finishing up a few writing commitments and settling into life in the small beach community of Tsawwassen, south of Vancouver, British Columbia, Canada. Wyn and I moved here when I retired, in part to be closer to our daughter and her family, but also to enjoy the conveniences and slower pace of a small town, something we both knew as children. Of course, as adolescents and young adults we were delighted to escape the familiarity and vigilance of small town life. But old age and small towns seem to go together nicely.

Gearing Down

I now find myself in the middle of an identity shift from scholar to one who dabbles occasionally in quasi-scholarly activities when being a grandfather, husband, friend, and attempting to stay physically active permit. Most of my dabbling thus far has been devoted to three projects—this memoir, the researching and writing of a work of general non-fiction entitled *Hometown Asylum*, and planning and outlining a biographical life positioning analysis of Canada's well-known former Prime Minister, Pierre Elliott Trudeau, father of our current Prime Minister, Justin Trudeau. For this last project, I still am in the "reading, studying, and annotating" phase. *Hometown Asylum* is a family memoir and history of the Alberta Hospital Ponoka, the large provincial psychiatric facility near the small Central Alberta town of Ponoka where I grew up. My paternal grandmother was a patient at the hospital, my father worked at the hospital as a baker, and I and several of my friends worked there as institutional attendants. In working on *Hometown Asylum*, I am discovering that writing nonfiction for a general audience requires a very different "skillset" from that required for writing and publishing scholarly, academic articles, and books. Time will tell whether or not I can make the jump. Since obtaining a publishing contract from Routledge, the writing of this autobiographical memoir has been my primary pursuit—one that turns out to have involved much more fact checking and document searching than I imagined it would.

To maintain some contact with professional and academic friends and acquaintances, I continue to serve on the editorial boards of the *Journal of Theoretical and Philosophical Psychology* and *Theory & Psychology*. I also joined Brent Slife and others on the editorial board of Brent's book series, *Advances in Theoretical and Philosophical Psychology*, commissioned by Lucy McClune at Routledge. This memoir is published in that series. Brent is a well-known and respected psychologist who has given freely of his time and energies in support of theoretical psychology and psychology in general. Over the years, I have benefitted greatly from his counsel and generosity in supporting my efforts to move toward a psychology of persons. When I was about to give up on publishing my biographical essay on Skinner and Rogers (Martin, 2017), Brent, in his capacity as editor of the *Journal of Theoretical and Philosophical Psychology*, came to my assistance. I owe a great debt to Brent and other members of the Society of Theoretical and Philosophical Psychology. Conversations with colleagues at the annual meetings of that society have stimulated and sustained my work on the psychology of personhood, demonstrating once again the never-ending richness of interactions with others for one's personal development. Even (and sometimes especially) when we disagree, these conversations have sustained me and deepened and extended my work.

We tend to think we are experts about our own lives. However, reconstructing a life is not straightforward. Even a brief memoir of a portion of one's life, such as what I am writing here, requires the recollection of events and experiences that may have grown fuzzy with, and been reconstructed, over time. All memoirs and autobiographies are necessarily perspectival, wedded as they are to their authors' inevitable interests and current sense of self and life. Selecting and focusing on some events and experiences inevitably obscure and modify others. Past events and happenings may be tailored, intentionally or inadvertently, to the narrative as it unfolds or to fit contemporary sensibilities of authors and their imagined audiences. The dynamic flow of any human life yields contradictions and ruptures that demand to be smoothed over to prevent the personal story from fracturing beyond the interpretive capacities of readers who also must rely on their own life experiences and perspectives to understand and interpret what they are reading. Social acceptability and legacy concerns add to this complex mix in ways that may be "caught," go undetected, or be sanctioned by authors.

Recently, a friend asked me if I ever have regretted foregoing conventional empirical research in psychology. I responded by saying that I have not. When asked why, I said that in my early career I kept hoping it might be possible to do psychological research in a way that was both more scientific and more informative. It was perhaps a vestige of this hope, in addition to obvious career ambitions, that helped me to persevere in the conduct of research on psychotherapeutic change during my time at the University of Western Ontario. However, toward the end of my time at Western, it was clear to me that what I really wanted to know about personhood, human agency, and the life experiences of myself and others was not going to come from engaging in psychological research alone. I needed to find additional ways of probing human existence and the human condition that could illuminate what it is to be a person.

Life Writing as a Primary Source and Method for a Psychology of Persons

Even while continuing to conduct counseling and psychotherapy research at Western, my reading was more and more in the theory and history of psychology, with a particular focus on personal being and agency. In the outpouring of books, chapters, and articles on these topics that followed my return to Simon Fraser, I explored ways of thinking about persons, their development, and their lives from a variety of philosophical and psychological perspectives, including those of hermeneutic, existential, and pragmatic philosophy and theoretical, sociocultural, developmental, and critical psychology. With Jeff Sugarman and others, I developed the theoretical framework for conceptualizing and understanding persons described in the previous and initial chapters of this book. All of this was very involving and rewarding.

Nonetheless, by 2010 I had grown weary of the abstracted nature of theoretical inquiry and was increasingly drawn to person-relevant studies and writings of historians of psychology like Kurt Danziger (1990) and Ian Hacking (1995) and to the life stories of psychologists and others. I found myself devouring biographies, autobiographies, and psychobiographies at an increasing rate. I always had been a fan of the genre, but I now saw more clearly how such writings provide concrete particulars about the lives of persons against which readers like myself can't help but consider our own life experiences and personhood.

I mostly had given up conventional empirical work by this time. Standard experimental and statistical studies in psychology no longer held much interest for me, especially when disconnected from particular persons and their lives. I no longer felt motivated to read widely in research journals. In stark contrast, life writings like biographies and autobiographies, with their detailed narratives of particular lives (as actually lived within specific historical periods and sociocultural contexts) gathered rapidly on my shelves. Instead of being limited by what can be studied easily by the scientific methods of psychology, such studies sampled directly the wide range and variety of life possibilities and constraints that can unfold and be enacted within the human condition, in all its diversity—an existential context that commands us somehow to realize and make sense of our personhood and find meaning in our lives. I saw how a close study of the lives and life experiences of particular persons could further the more general understandings of personal existence, psychological development, agency, meaning, and purpose that I and others had attempted to theorize. I began to view such works as a richly textured resource for comprehending what it is to be a person and to live the life of a person, exactly what I wanted for myself and imagined as intellectually and morally satisfying for others.

Immersing myself in life writings confirmed for me that it is persons and their lives that should matter most to psychology, especially to applied psychology. Psychology should offer possibilities for living as persons in full, not reductions and dissections of purportedly inner psychological structures and processes of dubious ontological status, especially when the findings gained are treated as applying to anyone in need of psychological understanding or assistance, in the absence of careful consideration of particular life circumstances. Many contemporaries turn to psychology for an understanding of themselves and their life experiences with others. The reductive individualism and focus on "inner causes" that are endemic and institutionalized in much empirical research in psychology increasingly struck me as inimical to the moral and social obligations implicit in offering supposedly scientifically-based professional treatments to particular persons, often without much detailed understanding of, or regard for, their life situations.

My life as a psychologist has involved freeing myself as much as I can from what I now regard as the scientistic sympathies that marked the early years of my career and demanded that I park my life experience at the doorstep of conventional experimental and quantitative inquiry. Why did I think for so long that psychology had to be solely scientific to be of any real value? Such a view is not scientific. Science does not dominate or exhaust all of human life. Our understanding and appreciation of life can be, and often are, enhanced greatly by studies, writings, performances, and creations in literature and the humanities, in aesthetics and the arts, in architecture and design, and in many other areas. As I write this, Jeff Sugarman and I have just published a new edited book that argues for and illustrates some of the many ways in which the humanities do and can continue to inform a viable psychology of persons and their lives (Sugarman & Martin, 2020). The overemphasis on science as the measure of all things is scientism not science. An over-valuing of science for all human purposes is mostly a function of factors unrelated to science per se, such as disciplinary turf wars, careerism and its attendant awards and anxieties, and the institutionalized indoctrination flowing through academic departments, scholarly and professional associations, and regulatory bodies.

Probably it is much easier for an old man to adopt an anti-scientistic attitude than a much younger person with a lifetime of professional and career struggles ahead. However, if psychology really is the discipline that more than any other reflects to us what we are and might become, restrictive and reductive scientism makes for a very inadequate, manipulated, and distorted mirror, especially if it is attended by instrumentalism and solipsistic individualism. I often told my students that if they really wanted to learn something new about themselves that might merit the time and energy of reflection to "look around, not inside."

As I approach the end of my career, I find myself drawn increasingly to the humanities for inspiration for, and examples of, the serious study of the person in full. Much of the concern of the humanities is not to be general but to be particular—to look closely at human lives and ways of living, to turn them about, to struggle to comprehend and "get a feel" for them—to walk through the landscape of particular lives and marvel over something unprecedented and unrepeatable therein.

> I have learned more from such particulars, more of what I can relate meaningfully to the human condition writ large, than I ever learned in the first twenty years of my professional life as a psychologist, during which time I was knee-deep in the conventional waters of empirical inquiry in general, educational, and psychotherapeutic psychology, yet seldom managed to achieve a genuinely "ah ha" moment.
>
> In contrast, in my biographical and psychobiographical studies, I have not only learned a great deal about the particular individuals I have studied, but I believe I have learned a great deal about myself and others, things that have changed me in what I regard as beneficial ways. By closely studying a few lives in detail, I have come to feel more connected to people in general. By interpreting and reflecting on the lives of others, I have come to understand and appreciate the very different ways in which it is possible to navigate major challenges of living, inevitable existential concerns, and the wonder and pain of close relationships.
>
> (Martin, 2020, p. 62)

I believe that psychobiographical inquiry and writing can enrich our understanding of ourselves and the human condition in ways that include but go well beyond disciplinary psychology. "It is only through an artistic, empathic synthesis that a genuine [understanding of life] emerges" (Stern, 1911, p. 329). Wilhelm Wundt, the founding father of experimental psychology, thought that rigorous psychological experimentation could apply only to the most basic of human responses and reactions and was convinced that such methods and approaches were powerless to probe and enhance our understanding of the everyday social interactions and lives of persons. Both Stern and Wundt recommended biography and other forms of life writing and study for understanding the vast majority of human functioning and experience. It was precisely such a realization that Sigmund Koch urged on psychologists many years later, pleading for them to "finally accept the circumstance that extensive and important sectors of psychological study require modes of inquiry rather more like those of the humanities than the sciences" (Koch, 1999, p. 416).

The Good and Evil Persons Do

I like to think that in the last half of my academic career I may have contributed to the development of a non-scientistic social psychology of the person, one that uses everyday observations, discourse, and life writing to understand people. I am fascinated by people—how and why we become what we are and do what we do. We are the most socially powerful and culturally capable beings on this planet. As such, we have enormous responsibility to safeguard not only our families, communities, and societies but also the biophysical world in which we exist and live. As persons, we can experience and exercise our subjectivity, sociality, and personal and collective agency in many ways, ways that can oscillate between good and evil. The question of what constitutes a good life always should be uppermost in our thinking and acting. Only persons can ask and probe such a question. Time will tell if we are up to the enormous challenges we face. It certainly will help if psychology can develop in ways that take us seriously by studying us as we are, with an eye to helping us consider carefully what we might become.

One of the things that retirement has provided me is more time to read and view works, productions, and documentaries in the arts, history, biography, cultural studies, and other areas of human endeavor that bear directly and indirectly on the theory, history, and practice of psychology. Margaretta Jolly (2017), in her mammoth two-volume *Encyclopedia of Life Writing*, recognizes "autobiographical and biographical forms" as the backbone of life writing, but also includes "under life writing's umbrella … testimony, artifacts, reminiscence, personal narrative, visual arts, photography, film, oral history" and related forms and modes of the genre (p. ix). Two recent examples that are indicative of the riches that film holds for a psychology of persons and their lives are the highly praised television series *Rectify*, and the documentary film *The Report*. I consider these two productions as wonderful examples of carefully and thoughtfully crafted, empirically-based inquiry into the actions and lives of persons that bear directly on psychological questions and issues concerning how we adjust to adversity and trauma and sometimes create them. Themes and instances of good and evil abound in both.

Rectify ran for four seasons from 2013–2016 and focuses on a man who at the age of 18 was wrongfully convicted of a rape and murder he did not commit, yet spent the next 20 years of his life on death row before being released when new evidence became available. The series examines in detail what happens when he is released, returns to his family and community, and tries to "catch up" on 20 years of familial, social, and technological change that has taken place during his time in prison. What I found so amazing about this production is that it made available to me problems, questions, and challenges I never would otherwise have considered, let alone understood—the magnitude of the difficulties he faced in adjusting to his life after so many years of incarceration, the complex, traumatic, and heart-rending ways in which his return affected him, members of his immediate family, and the lives of many others in his community. Years of occasionally hearing reports of people wrongfully imprisoned (including reading case files of and interacting with two people who had served prison sentences, one whom I encountered in my work as a psychiatric attendant and another I met as a fledgling psychotherapist) hadn't come anywhere close to informing me about the existential, psychological angst that unfolded as I watched this outstanding series. The same was true for a colleague who had taught courses to inmates as part of a university outreach program. The scholarly literature we had read and our limited personal experiences had been entirely insufficient in allowing us to grasp what we came to understand through the much more powerfully focused and emotionally immediate exposure to the realities of incarceration and its consequences portrayed in *Rectify*.

The Report is a 2019 dramatic film that depicts the CIA's use of torture in the aftermath of the September 11, 2001 attacks in New York, Shanksville, PA, and Washington, D.C. Despite having some general information about the involvement of the two clinical psychologists in the torture, I was shocked by the detailed and vivid portrayal of how Bruce Jessen and James Mitchell developed and advocated "enhanced interrogation techniques (EITs)" (including waterboarding, sleep deprivation, and methods of physical and sexual assault and humiliation that included "hooding, binding, and beating" and "rectal feeding"). These were methods that they taught, demonstrated, used, and encouraged others to use at various "black site" incarceration facilities at Abu Ghraib, Bagram, Guantanamo Bay, and elsewhere. Despite having no "intelligence" background or previous experience in conducting interrogations (although both had military backgrounds that included interrogations from military instructors as part of their training), Jessen and Mitchell received lucrative contracts for their work. Both psychologists claimed that the EITs they recommended and encouraged were based on psychological science, especially the theory of "learned helplessness." However, if so, "based on" must be given a very liberal reading.

Initial research on learned helplessness involved the electrical shocking of dogs, some of whom could not escape the shocks and eventually began to display "depressive" resignation to their plights (lying down and whining). Subsequent research with humans has tended to treat learned helplessness as a behavioral trait somewhat independent of contextual conditions, and has been conducted mostly in educational settings with those who display behaviors of "not trying," which have been interpreted as maladaptive and subjected to intervention and retraining. In these and other human studies, learned helplessness, now construed as "a feeling of lack of control," has been shown to vary greatly among different individuals and across different situations. It seems completely nonsensical and morally outrageous for Jessen and Mitchell to claim that psychological research on learned helplessness provides any kind of scientific basis or logical connection whatsoever for their despicable methods of "enhanced interrogation."

The Report, as a documentary film and form of life writing offers a vivid portrait of the ever-present possibility of human evil that lurks in the underbelly of human agency. Once others are deemed to be enemies, radically different from us, and threatening to our culture and ways of life, it can be shockingly easy to deny them the status of persons (Becker, 1973). When thus dehumanized, they seem to deserve to be humiliated and abused because of their actions and of what we imagine they might be capable.

One of the most dramatic simulations ever conducted by psychologists, which has been interpreted as demonstrating just how quickly and easily abusive actions can occur, is what has become known as Philip Zimbardo's Prison Study (Haney, Banks, Zimbardo, 1973), in which college students role-played prison guards and prisoners within a "prison set" constructed in the basement of Stanford University's Jordon Hall, the building that houses its Department of Psychology. Within six days, the students role-playing the guards became sufficiently abusive to their "prisoners" that the "experiment" had to be stopped. In a 2015 film, *The Stanford Prison Experiment*, Zimbardo himself is portrayed as becoming abusive to some of the student participants who were paid $15 a day to participate in the simulation.

Of course, the Stanford Prison study, and several others that have achieved wide-spread attention and a mix of acclaim and critical concern (like Stanley Milgram's studies of obedience), in no way constitute experiments in any formal sense. In my opinion, they are demonstrations of possible human actions and experience within psychologist-manufactured contexts that are assumed to be similar to particular historical and/or contemporary "real life" situations. However, if this is the case, I once again find myself asking why psychologists don't simply look to actual historical and/or contemporary records of human behavior as data sources rather than giving empirical and epistemic priority to their own simulations and quasi-experiments that only seem, in some very limited and peripheral ways, to resemble the real things.

In two replications of the Stanford Prison study (Lovibond, Mitherin, & Adams, 1979; Reicher & Haslam, 2006), there was no sadistic behavior or abuse on the part of the "guards" and none of the "prisoners" exhibited psychological distress. It also is worth noting that in the original Haney et al. Stanford study, there was no uniformity of bad behavior across all the "guards." Bartels (2015) examined how the Stanford study is reported in introductory psychology textbooks and found that there is no indication of variation in the behavior of "guards" in 75% of introductory textbooks and none of the books mentioned either of the replication studies.

Milgram's studies of obedience and Zimbardo's prison study are more like staged performances, simulations, and demonstrations of human possibilities than they are properly controlled scientific experiments. When the psychological phenomena of personhood are taken out of real life contexts, they are changed. Purely physical phenomena, at least in their essential features, do not display finely tuned situational selectivity and reactivity. They are atomistically rather than socioculturally constituted. Given the sociocultural constitution of persons within our life contexts, there are no good reasons or moral justifications to privilege data collected in the artificial scenarios and performance simulations that social psychologists have constructed over empirical data that can be drawn from the actual lives and experiences of people. Nowhere is this truer than with respect to the good and evil that persons do. These are matters to be faced directly in as much factual detail as possible. They are not matters for simulation that deflects our rational and ethical attention to morally irrelevant questions about what such made-up scenarios may or may not tell us.

Persons in Plain View

I think it important to make a clear distinction between what I, and others like Elmer Sprague (1999) and Svend Brinkmann (2018), consider to be a legitimate and genuine psychology of the person in contrast with what is available in contemporary cognitive psychology and cognitive neuroscience, now considered by many to be the epitome of psychological science. Sprague views this distinction as between "mindism" and "personism" (p.

ix). Mindism treats the mind as the human brain and other more vaguely specified, internal entities such as computational architectures or information processing modules and operations. In contrast, personism denies that the mind is a thing or can be equated with brain, computational, or information processing structures and functions. Whereas mentalists claim that psychological properties can be ascribed or attributed to the brain or other "mind things," personists insist on an active agent stance in which psychological attributes should be applied only to persons. For personists, it is persons acting within their relationships and contexts that must be considered to be "the prime psychological reality" (Brinkmann, 2018, p. 27). As Peter Hacker (2007) has argued, human capabilities like intelligence or creativity or morality are not locked in our brains or minds; they are manifest in us persons acting intelligently or creatively or morally. Memory is not reified in inner neurophysiological structures; it is displayed in the more or less accurate recollections of persons. It is persons, not our minds or brains, that experience, reason, and act.

In addition to being biophysical human beings, persons are self-interpreting, rational, and moral agents with a distinctive ontogeny and unique capabilities, dispositions, and moral, existential concerns. We are uniquely social beings who collectively create the sociocultural contexts, practices, and ways of life that constitute as us as purposeful, psychological actors and agents. Our life activities and experiences are significant and matter to us. Psychology and psychologists do not need to invent and reify mental structures, processes, and operations (such as personality traits, self-schemata, and information processing mechanisms) and develop special instruments and assessment protocols to "measure" such hypothesized entities so as to make aspects of our psychological being and comportment "visible." We (the persons that we are) already are in plain view, going about our daily lives and displaying all the capabilities and dispositions that define us as rational and moral agents in what we do and how we talk to each other about our doings.

A genuine philosophy and psychology of persons (what Sprague, 2019 has called "personism") is unfettered by the invention and manufacture of intrapersonal, causal entities, and other constructions of reductive scientism because it takes persons and their lives as its psychological subject matter. The mind is not a mental thing that can be studied scientifically; it is the capabilities and dispositions displayed by persons interacting with others within their life contexts. You and I are not our alleged psychological interiors or our biophysical brains. Our actions and experiences are not explained by purported representational, psychodynamic, or sub-personal structures and processes in unspecified and un-locatable, inner recesses. We have brains that are vital to what we do, but as vital as they are, it is not our brains that do and act. It is us—the persons we are. The first principle of personism is that psychological terms and psychology itself make sense only when applied to persons and how we live our lives.

Taking Stock of My Life in Psychology

Throughout this memoir, I have emphasized the close and dynamically unfolding relationship between persons and psychology. Psychological discourse, knowledge, and intervention provide descriptions and suggest ways of being and acting as a person. Psychology has become salient in the sociocultural constitution of persons. It is part of what "makes us up," to use Hacking's (2006) term of art. In this regard, I would be remiss if I did not emphasize some of the ways in which I believe my personhood has been formed by my participation in psychological discourse and practice. Like most psychologists I know, I do not hold with the sentiment once encouraged by scholarly and professional psychology to the effect that psychological theory and inquiry (scientific or otherwise) can or ought be removed from the interests and values of psychologists as persons.

When I transferred to the study of psychology as an undergraduate at the University of Alberta, I wanted to sample as much of it as I could. Somewhat later, I became attracted to (or perhaps distracted by) B. F. Skinner's psychology of behavioral control. Given my scientific penchant at the time, I was impressed by the procedural replicability of Skinner's operant conditioning methods, if one allowed for the obvious facts that different reinforcers worked for individual organisms at different times, and that this variety of individual and situational differences increased greatly for "human subjects." During my graduate studies, I became adept at applying principles drawn from applied behavioral analysis to shape and direct some of my own behaviors (e.g., scheduling and rewarding myself for time studied, pages written, and adherence to training regimens). My later interest in self-reinforcement and self-control, during my first stint at SFU, combined personal, professional, and scholarly interests. I understood behavioral self-control as a science-based, procedural technology that could be harnessed in the broader interests of personal development and used eclectically (in my case, with elements of psychodynamic and humanistic psychology) to understand and help change myself and others in ways we desired.

Both at SFU and UWO, I applied to my personal life some of the therapeutic theories, skills, and strategies I was teaching and studying in my research. I think to this day that I became a much better husband, father, and friend by adapting some of the clinical methods and attitudes I was immersed in professionally to my personal life. When I returned to SFU, my theoretical and historical studies of personhood and agency fit well with a personal agenda to understand my own life and the lives of those close to me more fully. My late-life study of life writing in general and biography and auto-biography in particular has allowed me to take stock of my life in order to understand the person I have become and the life I've led. This memoir is part of that ongoing process.

Over the course of my life as a psychologist, I have used psychology as a rich source of possibilities for personal and social development and existential perspective. My criticisms of scientific psychology are not intended to attack or dismantle what I have and continue to find valuable and useful in psychology. Early on, I was drawn to a technology of behavior modification and self-control that I perceived as scientifically based. Later, I benefited from adapting what I understood as useful clinical insights and ways of interacting to my personal relationships. More recently, I feel extremely fortunate to have more time to explore the vast literature of life writing more generally for ways of coming to grips with life and its inevitabilities. In many ways, professionally and personally, psychology has been and continues to be, for me, the most interesting "game in town." It is not scientific or even disciplinary psychology I crave, but psychology in the broad and general sense of understanding persons and the lives we live with the ideal of a good life in mind—a life Ernest Becker described in his "ideal/real theory of democracy" as one in which each person strives to achieve "maximum individuality within maximum community" (as cited in Liechty, 2005, p. 19).

Given the great importance a psychology of persons attaches to the interpersonal, sociocultural, and material contexts of our lives, it is perhaps unsurprising that one of my most sustaining lines of thought as I enter the final phases of my life is to think of myself and all of us as "culture carriers and curators." I think this is a life role and purpose that is inescapable for all persons—past, present, and future. Personism places us and our lives at the center of psychology, as its primary focus. We are constituted as persons through our active participation within our life contexts with others. Thus constituted, we are able to act and collaborate in ways that add to the sociocultural, historical contexts experienced and lived by those who come after us. In this way, all of us are not only culture carriers and curators, but also (in some measure) culture creators. For my part, I will be well satisfied if my career work in psychology contributes in some small way to a more vibrant psychology of personhood—a psychology that is focused on understanding the persons we are and our lives as lived.

It was my desire to understand persons (myself and others) that first drew me to psychology. Being committed to science as a royal road to understanding in general, I struggled for many years to squeeze whatever relevant insights I could from scientific research in psychology, despite my growing skepticism about the scientific status of such research. What I finally realized was that what I was looking for was right in front of me all along: persons doing what we do in our lives. There is no need to invent models and theories of psyches and minds, formulate behavioral contingencies and schedules based on research with non-person animals, or construct special research scenarios, procedures, and instruments to capture and probe us. Sometimes the practices of science pay huge dividends; sometimes they do as much or even more to obscure than they do to reveal. A great deal depends on whether or not the focus is on what matters in ways that don't distort it. In psychology, what matters is persons and what we do in and with our lives.

A Way Forward?

There is one matter frequently voiced by many students, colleagues, and others who are sympathetic to my later-career work on personhood and life writing. It combines a concern and a request. The concern is that if they were to do work of this kind, it would not be well received by many of their faculty colleagues or fellow students, editors of psychological journals, departmental chairs and supervisory committees, and review boards for granting agencies. The request is for help in finding ways of navigating this concern. The larger question, of course, is about the institutional culture of contemporary academic psychology.

In 1966, Marvin Dunnette, then President of Division 24 (Industrial and Organizational Psychology) of the American Psychological Association, critically commented on certain features of this culture as presenting major impediments to change.

> The whole Zeitgeist seems to encourage research efforts that earn big grants, crank out publications frequently and regularly, self-perpetuate themselves, don't entail much difficulty in getting subjects, don't require the researchers to move from behind their desks or out of their laboratories except to accept speaking engagements, and serve to protect the scientist from all forces that can knock him out of the secure "visible circle."
>
> (Dunnette, 1966, p. 360).

I think elements of the 1960s zeitgeist continue to be in evidence in most contemporary departments of psychology. However, I also think that alternatives are much more readily available now than when I entered the University of Alberta as a freshman the year after Dunnette's article appeared in the *American Psychologist*. Currently, there are signs that psychology, or at least a growing number of psychologists, is finally recognizing the potential of life writing for advancing its understanding of persons and the human condition. A ninth volume in the series *A History of Psychology in Autobiography* has been published. The flagship journal of the American Psychological Association, *American Psychologist*, recently published a special issue on psychobiography. A new society, the Society for Qualitative Research in Psychology, has been established and book series in narrative psychology have begun to appear (e.g., the Oxford series "Explorations in Narrative Psychology" edited by Mark Freeman). Of course, not all qualitative or narrative research in psychology or elsewhere focuses on individual persons within their particular life contexts, but there are increasing examples of work that does exactly this. Moreover, if any psychologist interested in life writing is willing to go beyond the borders of disciplinary psychology an extensive literature of life writing is readily available.

The kinds of experience I have described in this memoir, while obviously my own, are not unique to me. For example, Sigmund Koch, who also started his career as a devout behaviorist and later wrote extensively of his concerns about scientism and methodological orthodoxy in psychology (e.g., Koch, 1999), spent the last years of his career and life establishing an Aesthetics Research Center at Boston University. Established in January 1983, the initial aim of this institute was to recruit major artists (like playwright Edward Albee, novelist Saul Bellow, visual artist Mercedes Matter, composer Milton Babbitt, poet Richard Wilbur, architect Edward Larabee Barnes, and ballerina Violette Verdi) to engage in four extended "research conversations" (each of two hours in duration) over two days. To prepare for these conversations, Koch immersed himself in "everything the artist had published or recorded, and in the critical and biographical literature bearing on the artist" (Koch, 1999, p. 45). Based on these "immersions" into the lives of the participating artists, Koch also prepared detailed sets of discussion themes that "were used flexibly and in no fixed order during a given discussion," with the aim of allowing for and inviting "organic development of each conversation." Importantly, "the artists were not 'subjects' ... but collaborators" who were "not interviewed but conversed" (p. 45). When these "conversational studies" with the various artist collaborators were written, they were formatted and organized into sections on "personal and professional development," "process and craft," and views on the historical and contemporary status of the artist's "field or genre." Koch commented that he, and "many competent viewers" he consulted, considered these written studies to be "among the richest sources of artist-generated information concerning their own working methods, objectives, value-systems, sensibility profiles in history" (p. 46). Among his interpretations was the expressed view "that artists are *not* a separate genus, but are *persons* who use in a special way faculties that all of us share." Koch also remarked that "I conducted myself as a *person*, not a psychologist in this work" (p. 47).

In the previous chapter, I mentioned the particular interest that many psychologists have shown in writing biographies and autobiographies.

The autobiographies of psychologists are rich resources for understanding psychology, its history, and its culture. In 2002, Darek Dawda, a doctoral student working with me, and I examined 73 full and partial autobiographies written by prominent psychologists in an attempt to understand better the reasons so many psychologists seemed not to acknowledge what we regarded as significant problems of reductionism in psychology. Derek and I concluded that there was a large gap between how these psychologists interpreted the significance of their work and the reductive methods they frequently employed in conducting their research, a gap we traced to their scholarly and professional education and socialization. In short, they were trained not to "attend to discrepancies between their conduct as researchers and their aspirations for understanding and explaining everyday human action and experience." Often, they rationalized their inattention by "the belief that science inevitably progresses from simple, basic formulations and experiments to more complex, advanced understandings and explanations" (Martin & Dawda, 2002, p. 40).

Biographical and autobiographical life writings and secondary analyses of them, certainly do not exhaust the range of life writing studies and methods already available in psychology. In addition, there are detailed examples of case and observational studies and reports in clinical psychology (e.g., Freud's case studies), developmental psychology (e.g., Piaget's observations of his children), physiological psychology (e.g., Broca's studies of Leborge, Lelong, and others with cerebral impairments), and the history of psychology (e.g., Hacking's study of "mad traveler" Albert Dadas). A variety of life writing methods also are routinely part of the work of many qualitative psychologists like Ruthellen Josselson, Dan McAdams, Mark Freeman, and Sunil Bhatia. There is no shortage of examples of life writing in psychology that might guide the would-be life writer and student of personhood (see Martin, 2020 for additional resources).

I think an important next step might be to attempt a modest extension to the curricula offered in most psychology departments to accommodate a course in historical biography and life writing. Such a course could expose students to the genre and its methods, and provide illustrative examples. Perhaps students could be helped to conduct somewhat detailed studies of a particular people and their lives using methods of life writing (to make such student projects feasible, the course I am suggesting should not be folded into a course on qualitative methods in general). Researching and writing assignments of this kind hopefully will help students to understand how a biographical understanding of a particular person's life differs from the understanding of persons that issues from more typical research methods in psychology. Direct experience of this difference can occasion reflection on how little we actually know about the participants in the vast majority of extant research in psychology. It is possible to survey and experiment in ways that are efficient and arguably useful for some of the purposes of psychology but such work, whatever its possible merits and applications, mostly cannot be said to inform us about ourselves, our lives, and our possibilities. Technical, procedural outcomes can be useful, but they should not govern or unduly limit or preempt our search for an adequate understanding of persons, lives, and the human condition.

I think the most important thing we psychologists can do is to avoid bringing an ontological detachment to our work as researchers and practitioners. In particular, we must be vigilant in guarding against an over-reliance on methodologies that can alienate us from ourselves. This is why I think it so important to focus on persons-in-context as irreducible ontological units of psychological inquiry and practice. If there is one thing the history of psychology teaches us, it is that ours is a discipline and profession that too often has allowed its methodologies to dictate what we study and how we study it. It is time for psychology to embrace the complexities of personhood with the purposes of understanding what we are and how we have come this far, while also envisioning the further purpose of contributing to human flourishing across our similarities and differences. Given the often recognized capacity of psychological thought and practice to figure significantly in the sociocultural, historical constitution of persons (cf. Hacking, 2006), we psychologists have an intellectual and moral obligation to do whatever we can to ensure that our creations and practices tend toward beneficence.

References

Bartels, J. M. (2015). The Stanford prison experiment in introductory psychology textbooks: A content analysis. *Psychology Learning and Teaching, 14*(1), 36–50.

Becker, E. (1973). *The denial of death.* New York: Free Press.

Brinkmann, S. (2018). *Persons and their minds: Towards an integrative theory of the mediated mind.* Abingdon, UK: Routledge.

Dunnette, M. D. (1966). Fads, fashions, and folderol in psychology. *American Psychologist, 21*(4), 343–352.

Hacker, P. M. S. (2007). *Human nature: The categorical framework.* London: Blackwell Publishing.

Hacking, I. (1995). *Rewriting the soul: Multiple personality and the sciences of memory.* Princeton, NJ: The University of Princeton Press.

Hacking, I. (2006). *Making up people.* London: London Review of Books, August 17 Issue.

Haney, C., Banks, C., & Zimbardo, P. (1973). Interpersonal dynamics in a simulated prison. *International Journal of Criminology and Penology, 1*, 69–97.

Jolly, M. (2017). *Encyclopedia of life writing: Autobiographical and biographical forms.* London: Routledge.

Koch, S. (1999). *Psychology in human context: Essays in dissidence and reconstruction* (D. Finkleman & F. Kessel, Eds.). Chicago, IL: The University of Chicago Press.

Liechty, D. (Ed.). (2005). *The Ernest Becker reader*. Seattle, WA: The Ernest Becker Foundation in association with The University of Washington Press.

Lovibond, S. H., Mithiran, X., & Adams, W. G. (1979). The effects of three experimental prison environments on the behavior of non-convict volunteer subjects. *Australian Psychologist, 14*(3), 273–287.

Martin, J. (2017). Carl Rogers' and B. F. Skinner's approaches to personal and societal improvement: A study in the psychological humanities. *Journal of Theoretical and Philosophical Psychology, 37*(4), 214–229.

Martin, J. (2020). Methods of life writing for a psychology of persons. In J. Sugarman & J. Martin (Eds.), *A humanities approach to the psychology of personhood* (pp. 49–64). New York: Routledge.

Martin, J., & Dawda, D. (2002). Reductionism in the comments and autobiographical accounts of prominent psychologists. *Journal of Psychology, 136*(1), 37–52.

Reicher, S., & Haslam, S. A. (2006). Rethinking the psychology of tyranny: The BBC prison study. *British Journal of Social Psychology, 45*(1), 1–40.

Sprague, E. (2019). *Persons and their minds: A philosophical investigation*. New York: Routledge.

Stern, W. (1911). *Die differentielle Psychologie in ihren methodischen Grundlagen* [*Methodological foundations of differential psychology*]. Leipzig: Barth.

Sugarman, J., & Martin, J. (2020). *A humanities approach to the psychology of personhood*. New York: Routledge.

Index